TEST PREP WORKBOOK

SIDE by SIDE

② Plus

Steven J. Molinsky • Bill Bliss

Side by Side Plus Test Prep Workbook 2

Pearson Education, 10 Bank Street, White Plains, NY 10606

Staff credits: The people who make up the *Side by Side Plus* team, representing content creation, design, manufacturing, marketing, multimedia, project management, publishing, rights management, and testing are Pietro Alongi, Allen Ascher, Rhea Banker, Elizabeth Barker, Lisa Bayrasli, Elizabeth Carlson, Jennifer Castro, Tracey Munz Cataldo, Diane Cipollone, Aerin Csigay, Victoria Denkus, Dave Dickey, Daniel Dwyer, Wanda España, Oliva Fernandez, Warren Fischbach, Pam Fishman, Nancy Flaggman, Patrice Fraccio, Irene Frankel, Aliza Greenblatt, Lester Holmes, Janet Johnston, Caroline Kasterine, Barry Katzen, Ray Keating, Renee Langan, Jaime Lieber, José Antonio Méndez, Julie Molnar, Alison Pei, Pamela Pia, Stuart Radcliffe, Jennifer Raspiller, Kriston Reinmuth, Mary Perrotta Rich, Tania Saiz-Sousa, Katherine Sullivan, Paula Van Ells, Kenneth Volcjak, Paula Williams, and Wendy Wolf.

Text composition: TSI Graphics, Inc.

Illustrations: Richard E. Hill

The authors gratefully acknowledge the contribution of Tina Carver in the development of the original *Side by Side* program.

ISBN-10: 0-13-418676-1
ISBN-13: 978-0-13-418676-4

Printed in the United States of America

1 2 3 4 5 6 7 8 9 10—V011—22 21 20 19 18 17 16 15

CONTENTS

PREFACE

Side by Side Plus Test Prep Workbook 2 provides unit achievement tests designed to reinforce and assess the learning objectives in *Side by Side Plus Student Book 2*. The tests provide focused coverage of lifeskill competencies and employment topics, assess student progress, and prepare students for the types of standardized tests and performance assessments used by many instructional programs. The content of each test is based on the grammar, vocabulary, and topics covered in the particular unit of the student book.

The achievement tests offer students practice with a variety of test-item formats:

- Multiple-choice questions assess vocabulary, grammar, reading, lifeskill and work-related competencies, and literacy tasks (such as reading medicine labels, signs, and everyday documents).
- Listening assessments offer practice with the types of listening comprehension tasks common in standardized tests.
- Writing assessments can be evaluated using a scoring rubric and collected in portfolios of students' work.
- Speaking performance assessments are designed to stimulate face-to-face interactions between students, for evaluation by the teacher using a standardized scoring rubric, or for self-evaluation by students. (The speaking assessments can also be used to evaluate students individually if time and resources allow for teachers or aides to conduct these assessments on a one-to-one basis.)

Test pages are perforated so that completed tests can be handed in and can serve as a record of students' participation and progress in the instructional program.

The Digital Audio CD included with the Workbook contains all listening activities in the achievement tests. You may choose to do these activities in class or have students complete them on their own using the audio. Listening scripts are provided in *Side by Side Plus Teacher's Guide 2*.

Side by Side Plus Multilevel Activity & Achievement Test Book 2 (included with the Teacher's Guide) provides test preparation strategies, answer keys, scoring rubrics, and resources for documenting students' progress—all in a volume of reproducible masters and an accompanying CD-ROM.

Name _____

Date _____ Class _____

A ASKING PERSONAL INFORMATION QUESTIONS

Choose the sentence with the same meaning.

Example:

What's your age?
- Ⓐ How tall are you?
- Ⓑ What's your weight?
- Ⓒ How old are you?
- Ⓓ Where were you born? Ⓐ Ⓑ ● Ⓓ

1. What's your date of birth?
- Ⓐ What country are you from?
- Ⓑ Where were you born?
- Ⓒ What's your marital status?
- Ⓓ When were you born?

2. What's your marital status?
- Ⓐ How much do you weigh?
- Ⓑ Are you married or single?
- Ⓒ What country are you from?
- Ⓓ How tall are you?

3. Where were you born?
- Ⓐ What's your height?
- Ⓑ What's your weight?
- Ⓒ What's your date of birth?
- Ⓓ What's your place of birth?

4. How tall are you?
- Ⓐ What's your height?
- Ⓑ What's your weight?
- Ⓒ What's your age?
- Ⓓ What's your nationality?

5. What country are you from?
- Ⓐ What's your marital status?
- Ⓑ When were you born?
- Ⓒ What's your nationality?
- Ⓓ Are you married or single?

B ANSWERING PERSONAL INFORMATION QUESTIONS

Choose the correct answer.

Example:

What's your zip code?
- Ⓐ 415.
- Ⓑ 10027.
- Ⓒ 027-48-9451.
- Ⓓ #12-G. Ⓐ ● Ⓒ Ⓓ

6. What's your telephone number?
- Ⓐ 283-73-2851.
- Ⓑ (215) 627-9382.
- Ⓒ 97623.
- Ⓓ 1267-B.

7. What's your height?
- Ⓐ 155 pounds.
- Ⓑ 27 years old.
- Ⓒ Five feet eight inches.
- Ⓓ Brown.

8. What's your nationality?
- Ⓐ Mexican.
- Ⓑ Los Angeles.
- Ⓒ California.
- Ⓓ Mexico City.

9. What's your weight?
- Ⓐ 22214.
- Ⓑ Five feet three inches.
- Ⓒ Married.
- Ⓓ 168 pounds.

10. What's your social security number?
- Ⓐ 124.
- Ⓑ 227-53-8716.
- Ⓒ (617) 372-9106.
- Ⓓ 33928.

1 Ⓐ Ⓑ Ⓒ Ⓓ   4 Ⓐ Ⓑ Ⓒ Ⓓ   7 Ⓐ Ⓑ Ⓒ Ⓓ   10 Ⓐ Ⓑ Ⓒ Ⓓ

2 Ⓐ Ⓑ Ⓒ Ⓓ   5 Ⓐ Ⓑ Ⓒ Ⓓ   8 Ⓐ Ⓑ Ⓒ Ⓓ

3 Ⓐ Ⓑ Ⓒ Ⓓ   6 Ⓐ Ⓑ Ⓒ Ⓓ   9 Ⓐ Ⓑ Ⓒ Ⓓ

Go to the next page ⟩

C PERSONAL INFORMATION FORM

```
Name:     (1) _____

Street:   (2) _____  Apartment: (3) _____

City:  (4) _____  State: (5) _____  Zip Code: (6) _____

Social Security Number:  (7) _____  Country of Origin:  (8) _____

Telephone:  (9) _____  E-Mail: (10) _____  Age:  (11) _____

Height:  (12) _____  Weight: (13) _____  Eye Color:  (14) _____  Hair Color:  (15) _____
```

Look at the information. Choose the correct line on the form.

Example:

#201-C
Ⓐ Line 1
Ⓑ Line 2
Ⓒ Line 3
Ⓓ Line 4   Ⓐ Ⓑ ● Ⓓ

11. 5479 Washington Boulevard
Ⓐ Line 2
Ⓑ Line 4
Ⓒ Line 8
Ⓓ Line 10

12. China
Ⓐ Line 1
Ⓑ Line 2
Ⓒ Line 8
Ⓓ Line 10

13. andre27@ail.com
Ⓐ Line 1
Ⓑ Line 6
Ⓒ Line 7
Ⓓ Line 10

14. 5 ft. 10 in.
Ⓐ Line 3
Ⓑ Line 12
Ⓒ Line 13
Ⓓ Line 14

15. blue
Ⓐ Line 12
Ⓑ Line 13
Ⓒ Line 14
Ⓓ Line 15

11 Ⓐ Ⓑ Ⓒ Ⓓ   13 Ⓐ Ⓑ Ⓒ Ⓓ   15 Ⓐ Ⓑ Ⓒ Ⓓ
12 Ⓐ Ⓑ Ⓒ Ⓓ   14 Ⓐ Ⓑ Ⓒ Ⓓ

Go to the next page ⟩

Name _____ Date _____

Choose the correct answer to complete the conversation.

Example:

What's your _____?

Ⓐ city
Ⓑ nationality
Ⓒ height
● name

16. My name _____ Marie Isabel Fuentes.

Ⓐ am
Ⓑ is
Ⓒ are
Ⓓ call

17. _____ do you spell your last name?

Ⓐ How
Ⓑ Who
Ⓒ Where
Ⓓ Why

18. _____.

Ⓐ N-A-M-E
Ⓑ M-A-R-I-A
Ⓒ I-S-A-B-E-L
Ⓓ F-U-E-N-T-E-S

19. What's your _____ number?

Ⓐ zip
Ⓑ security
Ⓒ e-mail
Ⓓ telephone

20. My phone number is _____.

Ⓐ 20018
Ⓑ 317-29-7834
Ⓒ (627) 442-3862
Ⓓ #17-H

21. _____ are you from?

Ⓐ Where
Ⓑ When
Ⓒ Why
Ⓓ How

22. _____ from Guatemala.

Ⓐ I
Ⓑ I'm
Ⓒ My
Ⓓ You're

23. What's your _____?

Ⓐ age
Ⓑ weight
Ⓒ height
Ⓓ nationality

24. I'm five _____ four inches.

Ⓐ feet
Ⓑ pounds
Ⓒ tall
Ⓓ weigh

. . . .

16 Ⓐ Ⓑ Ⓒ Ⓓ   **19** Ⓐ Ⓑ Ⓒ Ⓓ   **22** Ⓐ Ⓑ Ⓒ Ⓓ

17 Ⓐ Ⓑ Ⓒ Ⓓ   **20** Ⓐ Ⓑ Ⓒ Ⓓ   **23** Ⓐ Ⓑ Ⓒ Ⓓ

18 Ⓐ Ⓑ Ⓒ Ⓓ   **21** Ⓐ Ⓑ Ⓒ Ⓓ   **24** Ⓐ Ⓑ Ⓒ Ⓓ

Go to the next page ⟹

Look at the calendar. Choose the correct answer.

2025

January						
S	M	T	W	T	F	S
				1	2	3	4
5	6	7	8	9	10	11
12	13	14	15	16	17	18
19	20	21	22	23	24	25
26	27	28	29	30	31	

February						
S	M	T	W	T	F	S
						1
2	3	4	5	6	7	8
9	10	11	12	13	14	15
16	17	18	19	20	21	22
23	24	25	26	27	28	

March						
S	M	T	W	T	F	S
						1
2	3	4	5	6	7	8
9	10	11	12	13	14	15
16	17	18	19	20	21	22
23/30	24/31	25	26	27	28	29

April						
S	M	T	W	T	F	S
		1	2	3	4	5
6	7	8	9	10	11	12
13	14	15	16	17	18	19
20	21	22	23	24	25	26
27	28	29	30			

May						
S	M	T	W	T	F	S
				1	2	3
4	5	6	7	8	9	10
11	12	13	14	15	16	17
18	19	20	21	22	23	24
25	26	27	28	29	30	31

June						
S	M	T	W	T	F	S
1	2	3	4	5	6	7
8	9	10	11	12	13	14
15	16	17	18	19	20	21
22	23	24	25	26	27	28
29	30				

July						
S	M	T	W	T	F	S
		1	2	3	4	5
6	7	8	9	10	11	12
13	14	15	16	17	18	19
20	21	22	23	24	25	26
27	28	29	30	31	

August						
S	M	T	W	T	F	S
					1	2
3	4	5	6	7	8	9
10	11	12	13	14	15	16
17	18	19	20	21	22	23
24/31	25	26	27	28	29	30

September						
S	M	T	W	T	F	S
	1	2	3	4	5	6
7	8	9	10	11	12	13
14	15	16	17	18	19	20
21	22	23	24	25	26	27
28	29	30				

October						
S	M	T	W	T	F	S
			1	2	3	4
5	6	7	8	9	10	11
12	13	14	15	16	17	18
19	20	21	22	23	24	25
26	27	28	29	30	31	

November						
S	M	T	W	T	F	S
						1
2	3	4	5	6	7	8
9	10	11	12	13	14	15
16	17	18	19	20	21	22
23/30	24	25	26	27	28	29

December						
S	M	T	W	T	F	S
	1	2	3	4	5	6
7	8	9	10	11	12	13
14	15	16	17	18	19	20
21	22	23	24	25	26	27
28	29	30	31			

Example:

Today is September 3rd. Today is _____.

Ⓐ Monday
Ⓑ Wednesday
Ⓒ Thursday
Ⓓ Saturday 　Ⓐ ● Ⓒ Ⓓ

25. My birthday is March 13th. This year my birthday is on a _____.

Ⓐ Monday
Ⓑ Sunday
Ⓒ Tuesday
Ⓓ Thursday

26. My father's birthday is December 22nd. This year his birthday is on a _____.

Ⓐ Sunday
Ⓑ Monday
Ⓒ Wednesday
Ⓓ Saturday

27. I'm going to start a new job on the first Monday in May. My first day of work is _____.

Ⓐ May 1st
Ⓑ May 2nd
Ⓒ May 5th
Ⓓ May 26th

28. The twelfth day of March this year is on a _____.

Ⓐ Wednesday
Ⓑ Saturday
Ⓒ Sunday
Ⓓ Thursday

29. My sister is going to get married on the second Saturday in June. The wedding is on _____.

Ⓐ June 7th
Ⓑ June 8th
Ⓒ June 14th
Ⓓ June 15th

F CLOZE READING: Providing Information About Family Members

Choose the correct answers to complete the story.

There are six people in my family. My father **is am are** a cashier. He
● Ⓑ Ⓒ

work works working 30 in a supermarket. My mother is **a an the** 31 teacher.
Ⓐ Ⓑ Ⓒ / Ⓐ Ⓑ Ⓒ

She He It 32 works in a pre-school. My sister is **with in from** 33 college. She's
Ⓐ Ⓑ Ⓒ / Ⓐ Ⓑ Ⓒ

study studies studying 34 medicine. I have two **brother brother's brothers** 35. One
Ⓐ Ⓑ Ⓒ / Ⓐ Ⓑ Ⓒ

brother is eight years old. He's in **high elementary middle** 36 school. The other brother is
Ⓐ Ⓑ Ⓒ

sixteen years old. He's in **high elementary middle** 37 school.
Ⓐ Ⓑ Ⓒ

G LISTENING ASSESSMENT: Giving Personal Information

Read and listen to the questions. Then listen to the interview and answer the questions.

38. What's his address?
- Ⓐ 19 Reedville Street.
- Ⓑ 94 Reedville Street.
- Ⓒ 419 Center Street.
- Ⓓ 94 Center Street.

39. When is his birthday?
- Ⓐ May 3rd.
- Ⓑ May 13th.
- Ⓒ May 30th.
- Ⓓ May 31st.

40. How tall is he?
- Ⓐ 5 feet 3 inches.
- Ⓑ 8 feet 5 inches.
- Ⓒ 5 feet 8 inches.
- Ⓓ 5 feet 10 inches.

H MONTHS, DAYS, & DATES

Look at the abbreviation. Write the correct month of the year.

NOV ____November____   JUL _____   JAN _____

AUG _____   JUN _____   FEB _____

MAR _____   APR _____   MAY _____

SEP _____   OCT _____   DEC _____

Look at the abbreviation. Write the correct day of the week.

MON _____   FRI _____   SUN _____

WED _____   SAT _____   TUE _____

THU _____

Write today's date. _____   **Write your date of birth.** _____

- -

30 Ⓐ Ⓑ Ⓒ Ⓓ	**33** Ⓐ Ⓑ Ⓒ Ⓓ	**36** Ⓐ Ⓑ Ⓒ Ⓓ	**39** Ⓐ Ⓑ Ⓒ Ⓓ
31 Ⓐ Ⓑ Ⓒ Ⓓ	**34** Ⓐ Ⓑ Ⓒ Ⓓ	**37** Ⓐ Ⓑ Ⓒ Ⓓ	**40** Ⓐ Ⓑ Ⓒ Ⓓ
32 Ⓐ Ⓑ Ⓒ Ⓓ	**35** Ⓐ Ⓑ Ⓒ Ⓓ	**38** Ⓐ Ⓑ Ⓒ Ⓓ	Go to the next page ⟩

I ORDINAL NUMBERS

Write the correct ordinal number.   **Write the correct word.**

second _____2nd_____   seventeenth _____   6th _____sixth_____

ninth _____   thirty-first _____   15th _____

first _____   fifty-third _____   21st _____

twelfth _____   eighty-fifth _____   92nd _____

J WRITING ASSESSMENT: Personal Information Form

Fill out the form.

Name: _____

Street: _____ Apartment: _____

City: _____ State: _____ Zip Code: _____

Telephone: _____ E-Mail: _____

Height: _____ Age: _____ Date of Birth: _____ Social Security Number: _____

Hair Color: _____ Eye Color: _____ Country of Origin: _____

Signature: _____ Today's Date: _____

K SPEAKING ASSESSMENT

I can ask and answer these questions:

Ask Answer

☐ ☐ What's your name?
☐ ☐ What's your address?
☐ ☐ What's your telephone number?
☐ ☐ What's your age?
☐ ☐ What's your date of birth?

Ask Answer

☐ ☐ Where are you from?
☐ ☐ What's your social security number?
☐ ☐ What's your height?
☐ ☐ Who are the people in your family?
☐ ☐ What do they do?

6

Name _____

Date _____ **Class** _____

2

A SCHOOL PERSONNEL & LOCATIONS

Choose the correct answer.

Example:

The _____ is in the classroom.
- Ⓐ custodian
- ● teacher
- Ⓒ security officer
- Ⓓ clerk

1. The _____ is in the library.
- Ⓐ principal
- Ⓑ security officer
- Ⓒ librarian
- Ⓓ science teacher

2. Our _____ is in the chemistry lab.
- Ⓐ science teacher
- Ⓑ English teacher
- Ⓒ music teacher
- Ⓓ school nurse

3. The _____ is in her office.
- Ⓐ driver's ed instructor
- Ⓑ librarian
- Ⓒ security officer
- Ⓓ principal

4. The _____ is in the cafeteria.
- Ⓐ music teacher
- Ⓑ custodian
- Ⓒ clerk
- Ⓓ security officer

5. The _____ is on the field.
- Ⓐ principal
- Ⓑ school nurse
- Ⓒ P.E. teacher
- Ⓓ science teacher

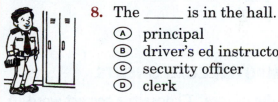
6. The _____ is in his office.
- Ⓐ librarian
- Ⓑ school nurse
- Ⓒ clerk
- Ⓓ guidance counselor

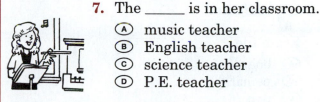
7. The _____ is in her classroom.
- Ⓐ music teacher
- Ⓑ English teacher
- Ⓒ science teacher
- Ⓓ P.E. teacher

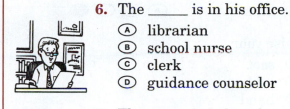
8. The _____ is in the hall.
- Ⓐ principal
- Ⓑ driver's ed instructor
- Ⓒ security officer
- Ⓓ clerk

9. The _____ is in the parking lot.
- Ⓐ P.E. teacher
- Ⓑ driver's ed instructor
- Ⓒ guidance counselor
- Ⓓ security officer

10. The _____ is in the school office.
- Ⓐ teacher
- Ⓑ school nurse
- Ⓒ security guard
- Ⓓ clerk

11. Our _____ is in our classroom.
- Ⓐ music teacher
- Ⓑ English teacher
- Ⓒ math teacher
- Ⓓ science teacher

B CLASSROOM INSTRUCTIONS

Choose the correct answer.

Example:

Open your _____.

- Ⓐ ruler
- Ⓑ pencil
- Ⓒ wall
- Ⓓ book   Ⓐ Ⓑ Ⓒ ●

12. Raise your _____.

- Ⓐ seat
- Ⓑ book
- Ⓒ hand
- Ⓓ computer

13. Erase the _____.

- Ⓐ board
- Ⓑ pencil
- Ⓒ pen
- Ⓓ globe

14. Take out a piece of _____.

- Ⓐ map
- Ⓑ dictionary
- Ⓒ book
- Ⓓ paper

15. Please hand in your _____.

- Ⓐ homework
- Ⓑ hand
- Ⓒ chair
- Ⓓ desk

16. Turn off the _____.

- Ⓐ map
- Ⓑ lights
- Ⓒ notebook
- Ⓓ ruler

C COMPUTER COMPONENTS

Look at the picture. Choose the correct word.

17.
- Ⓐ radio
- Ⓑ television
- Ⓒ monitor
- Ⓓ video

18.
- Ⓐ printer
- Ⓑ dictionary
- Ⓒ typewriter
- Ⓓ keyboard

19.
- Ⓐ notebook
- Ⓑ printer
- Ⓒ bookcase
- Ⓓ desk

20.
- Ⓐ mouse
- Ⓑ keyboard
- Ⓒ globe
- Ⓓ map

---

12 Ⓐ Ⓑ Ⓒ Ⓓ   15 Ⓐ Ⓑ Ⓒ Ⓓ   18 Ⓐ Ⓑ Ⓒ Ⓓ

13 Ⓐ Ⓑ Ⓒ Ⓓ   16 Ⓐ Ⓑ Ⓒ Ⓓ   19 Ⓐ Ⓑ Ⓒ Ⓓ

14 Ⓐ Ⓑ Ⓒ Ⓓ   17 Ⓐ Ⓑ Ⓒ Ⓓ   20 Ⓐ Ⓑ Ⓒ Ⓓ

Go to the next page ➤

D GRAMMAR IN CONTEXT: School Registration

Choose the correct answer to complete the conversation.

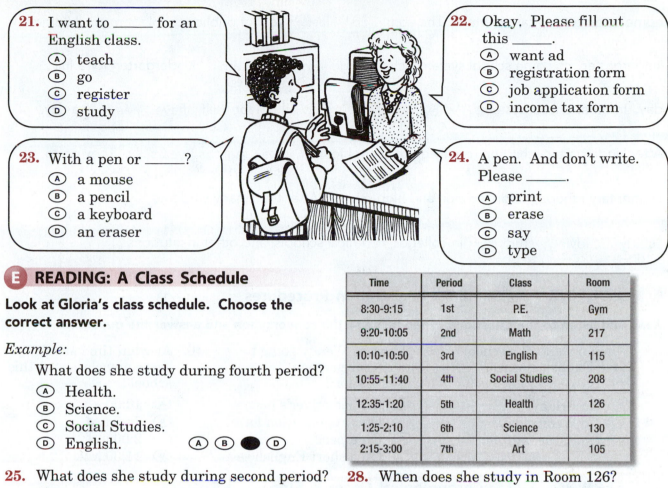

21. I want to _____ for an English class.
- Ⓐ teach
- Ⓑ go
- Ⓒ register
- Ⓓ study

22. Okay. Please fill out this _____.
- Ⓐ want ad
- Ⓑ registration form
- Ⓒ job application form
- Ⓓ income tax form

23. With a pen or _____?
- Ⓐ a mouse
- Ⓑ a pencil
- Ⓒ a keyboard
- Ⓓ an eraser

24. A pen. And don't write. Please _____.
- Ⓐ print
- Ⓑ erase
- Ⓒ say
- Ⓓ type

E READING: A Class Schedule

Look at Gloria's class schedule. Choose the correct answer.

Time	Period	Class	Room
8:30-9:15	1st	P.E.	Gym
9:20-10:05	2nd	Math	217
10:10-10:50	3rd	English	115
10:55-11:40	4th	Social Studies	208
12:35-1:20	5th	Health	126
1:25-2:10	6th	Science	130
2:15-3:00	7th	Art	105

Example:

What does she study during fourth period?
- Ⓐ Health.
- Ⓑ Science.
- Ⓒ Social Studies.
- Ⓓ English.   Ⓐ Ⓑ ● Ⓓ

25. What does she study during second period?
- Ⓐ P.E.
- Ⓑ Health.
- Ⓒ Art.
- Ⓓ Math.

26. It's 2:00. What's she studying?
- Ⓐ Social Studies.
- Ⓑ English.
- Ⓒ Science.
- Ⓓ Health.

27. It's 10:30. Where is she?
- Ⓐ In Room 115.
- Ⓑ In the gym.
- Ⓒ In Room 130.
- Ⓓ In Room 105.

28. When does she study in Room 126?
- Ⓐ Third period.
- Ⓑ Fifth perod.
- Ⓒ Sixth period.
- Ⓓ Seventh period.

29. What time does her Science class begin?
- Ⓐ At 8:30.
- Ⓑ At 2:10.
- Ⓒ At 1:25.
- Ⓓ At 1:30.

30. What time does her 7th period class end?
- Ⓐ At 9:15.
- Ⓑ At 2:15.
- Ⓒ In Room 105.
- Ⓓ At 3:00.

- -

21 Ⓐ Ⓑ Ⓒ Ⓓ   24 Ⓐ Ⓑ Ⓒ Ⓓ   27 Ⓐ Ⓑ Ⓒ Ⓓ   30 Ⓐ Ⓑ Ⓒ Ⓓ

22 Ⓐ Ⓑ Ⓒ Ⓓ   25 Ⓐ Ⓑ Ⓒ Ⓓ   28 Ⓐ Ⓑ Ⓒ Ⓓ

23 Ⓐ Ⓑ Ⓒ Ⓓ   26 Ⓐ Ⓑ Ⓒ Ⓓ   29 Ⓐ Ⓑ Ⓒ Ⓓ   Go to the next page ➡   **9** ●

F CLOZE READING: The Education System

There are many kinds of schools in the education system of the United States. Many young children go goes going to pre-school, but other children stayed stays stay [31] home or go to day-care centers. The one first last [32] year of public school for most children is kindergarten. In some school systems, children go from to with [33] kindergarten for a full day. In other school systems, they we I [34] go to school for half have heavy [35] a day. After kindergarten, children usually go to school for 12 days months years [36]. They go to elementary school, middle school, and high school. After that, many students study studying studies [37] in colleges, technical schools, and other institutions.

G LISTENING ASSESSMENT: Registration Procedures

Read and listen to the questions. Then listen to the conversation and answer the questions.

38. When DOESN'T the school have English classes?
   (A) On Monday.
   (B) On Friday.
   (C) On Wednesday.
   (D) On Saturday.

39. Where is Wendy going to write her personal information?
   (A) On her driver's license.
   (B) On a registration form.
   (C) On a pen.
   (D) On a short English test.

40. At what time AREN'T there any classes at this school?
   (A) 10:00 A.M.
   (B) 7:30 P.M.
   (C) 2:00 P.M.
   (D) 11:30 A.M.

H LEARNING SKILLS: Chronological Order & Steps in a Process

Put the classroom instructions in order.

_____ Write the answer.
_____ Sit down.
__1__ Stand up.
_____ Pick up the chalk.
_____ Go to the board.
_____ Put down the chalk.

Put the computer operations in order.

_____ Do your work.
_____ Insert the software disk.
_____ Eject the disk and turn off the computer.
_____ Open the software program.
_____ Save your work and close the program.
__1__ Turn on the computer.

I WRITING ASSESSMENT

Describe your school. Tell about the people, the classrooms, and other locations. (Use a separate sheet of paper.)

J SPEAKING ASSESSMENT

I can ask and answer these questions:

Ask Answer
☐ ☐ Where is our classroom?
☐ ☐ What's our class schedule?

. . . .

31 (A) (B) (C) (D)   34 (A) (B) (C) (D)   37 (A) (B) (C) (D)   40 (A) (B) (C) (D)

32 (A) (B) (C) (D)   35 (A) (B) (C) (D)   38 (A) (B) (C) (D)

● 10   33 (A) (B) (C) (D)   36 (A) (B) (C) (D)   39 (A) (B) (C) (D)

STOP

A FOOD CONTAINERS & QUANTITIES

Example:

We need a _____ of jam.

- Ⓐ box
- Ⓑ loaf
- ● jar
- Ⓓ bag

1. Please get a _____ of white bread.

- Ⓐ loaf
- Ⓑ bunch
- Ⓒ quart
- Ⓓ bottle

2. I'm looking for a _____ of flour.

- Ⓐ pint
- Ⓑ head
- Ⓒ loaf
- Ⓓ bag

3. I need two _____ of whole wheat bread.

- Ⓐ loaf
- Ⓑ loaves
- Ⓒ heads
- Ⓓ boxes

4. I need a _____ eggs.

- Ⓐ box
- Ⓑ twelve
- Ⓒ dozen
- Ⓓ pound

5. Please give me a _____ of cheese.

- Ⓐ can
- Ⓑ gallon
- Ⓒ pint
- Ⓓ pound

B FOOD WEIGHTS & MEASURES: Abbreviations

6. gal.

- Ⓐ quart
- Ⓑ pound
- Ⓒ gallon
- Ⓓ ounce

7. oz.

- Ⓐ ounce
- Ⓑ quart
- Ⓒ pound
- Ⓓ pounds

8. qt.

- Ⓐ pound
- Ⓑ pounds
- Ⓒ quart
- Ⓓ quarts

9. lbs.

- Ⓐ pound
- Ⓑ pounds
- Ⓒ quart
- Ⓓ quarts

10. ounces

- Ⓐ ozs.
- Ⓑ oz.
- Ⓒ lb.
- Ⓓ lbs.

11. pound

- Ⓐ gal.
- Ⓑ qt.
- Ⓒ lbs.
- Ⓓ lb.

C GRAMMAR IN CONTEXT: Asking About Availability & Location of Items in a Store

12. _____ any bananas today?

- Ⓐ Is there
- Ⓑ Are there
- Ⓒ There is
- Ⓓ There are

13. Yes. _____ in the Produce section.

- Ⓐ It
- Ⓑ It's
- Ⓒ They
- Ⓓ They're

14. Excuse me. _____ the milk?

- Ⓐ Have
- Ⓑ Where
- Ⓒ Where's
- Ⓓ Where are

15. _____ in the Dairy section.

- Ⓐ It's
- Ⓑ It
- Ⓒ They're
- Ⓓ They

1 Ⓐ Ⓑ Ⓒ Ⓓ   5 Ⓐ Ⓑ Ⓒ Ⓓ   9 Ⓐ Ⓑ Ⓒ Ⓓ   13 Ⓐ Ⓑ Ⓒ Ⓓ

2 Ⓐ Ⓑ Ⓒ Ⓓ   6 Ⓐ Ⓑ Ⓒ Ⓓ   10 Ⓐ Ⓑ Ⓒ Ⓓ   14 Ⓐ Ⓑ Ⓒ Ⓓ

3 Ⓐ Ⓑ Ⓒ Ⓓ   7 Ⓐ Ⓑ Ⓒ Ⓓ   11 Ⓐ Ⓑ Ⓒ Ⓓ   15 Ⓐ Ⓑ Ⓒ Ⓓ

4 Ⓐ Ⓑ Ⓒ Ⓓ   8 Ⓐ Ⓑ Ⓒ Ⓓ   12 Ⓐ Ⓑ Ⓒ Ⓓ   Go to the next page ⟩ **11**

Look at the food advertisements. Choose the correct answer.

16. How much are four heads of lettuce?
    - Ⓐ $2.00.
    - Ⓑ $3.00.
    - Ⓒ $4.00.
    - Ⓓ $8.00.

17. How much is half a pound of Swiss cheese?
    - Ⓐ $17.00.
    - Ⓑ $2.50.
    - Ⓒ $4.25.
    - Ⓓ $8.50.

18. How much are two pounds of Swiss cheese?
    - Ⓐ $8.50.
    - Ⓑ $17.00.
    - Ⓒ $4.25.
    - Ⓓ $2.00.

19. How much are four oranges?
    - Ⓐ $2.00.
    - Ⓑ $1.00.
    - Ⓒ $8.00.
    - Ⓓ $4.00.

20. How much are a dozen oranges?
    - Ⓐ $1.00.
    - Ⓑ $2.00.
    - Ⓒ $6.00.
    - Ⓓ $12.00.

21. How much are two bottles of apple juice?
    - Ⓐ Free.
    - Ⓑ $1.75.
    - Ⓒ $6.98.
    - Ⓓ $3.49.

16 Ⓐ Ⓑ Ⓒ Ⓓ   18 Ⓐ Ⓑ Ⓒ Ⓓ   20 Ⓐ Ⓑ Ⓒ Ⓓ

17 Ⓐ Ⓑ Ⓒ Ⓓ   19 Ⓐ Ⓑ Ⓒ Ⓓ   21 Ⓐ Ⓑ Ⓒ Ⓓ

Go to the next page ⟹

E READING: Food Packaging & Label Information

For each sentence, choose the correct label.

SELL BY MAR 04	Keep Refrigerated	Serving Size 1 cup (240g) Servings Per Container about 2	Center Pops Up When Original Seal Is Broken
A	B	C	D

22. Do not store at room temperature.
    Ⓐ Ⓑ Ⓒ Ⓓ

23. Contains 2 cups (480g).
    Ⓐ Ⓑ Ⓒ Ⓓ

24. Do not purchase if safety button is up.
    Ⓐ Ⓑ Ⓒ Ⓓ

25. Do not buy after this date.
    Ⓐ Ⓑ Ⓒ Ⓓ

F READING: A Supermarket Receipt

Look at the receipt. Choose the correct answer.

26. How much did the eggs cost?
    Ⓐ $2.69.   Ⓒ $2.10.
    Ⓑ $2.00.   Ⓓ $3.00.

27. How many bottles of soda did the person buy?
    Ⓐ One.   Ⓒ Three.
    Ⓑ Two.   Ⓓ Four.

28. How much did the person spend on soda?
    Ⓐ $2.00.   Ⓒ $1.00.
    Ⓑ $3.00.   Ⓓ $6.00.

29. How much does one loaf of bread cost?
    Ⓐ $1.00.   Ⓒ $3.00.
    Ⓑ $2.00.   Ⓓ $6.00.

30. How much do oranges cost at this supermarket?
    Ⓐ $3.00.   Ⓒ 12 for $4.00.
    Ⓑ 3 for $4.00.   Ⓓ 4 for $1.00.

31. How much did the person spend?
    Ⓐ $473.00.   Ⓒ $22.04.
    Ⓑ $2.96.   Ⓓ $25.00.

```
JUMBO SUPERMARKET #473

   LARGE EGGS        2.10
   MILK              2.69
   JAM               3.25
2 @ $1.00
   SODA              2.00
3 @ $2.00
   BREAD             6.00
2 @ 2 for $3.00
   LETTUCE           3.00
12 @ 4 for $1.00
   ORANGES           3.00

   TOTAL          $ 22.04
   TENDER         $ 25.00
   CHANGE         $  2.96

Thanks for shopping at JUMBO!
```

22 Ⓐ Ⓑ Ⓒ Ⓓ   25 Ⓐ Ⓑ Ⓒ Ⓓ   28 Ⓐ Ⓑ Ⓒ Ⓓ   31 Ⓐ Ⓑ Ⓒ Ⓓ

23 Ⓐ Ⓑ Ⓒ Ⓓ   26 Ⓐ Ⓑ Ⓒ Ⓓ   29 Ⓐ Ⓑ Ⓒ Ⓓ

24 Ⓐ Ⓑ Ⓒ Ⓓ   27 Ⓐ Ⓑ Ⓒ Ⓓ   30 Ⓐ Ⓑ Ⓒ Ⓓ

Go to the next page ⟹

G READING: Reading a Menu & Computing Costs

Look at the menu. Choose the correct answer.

SAMMY'S CAFE

SOUP

Vegetable Soup	Cup	1.50	Bowl	2.50
Onion Soup		2.00		3.00

SALAD

Tossed Salad   Small   1.50   Large   3.00

SIDE DISHES

French Fries	2.50	Carrots	2.00	
Rice	3.00	Peas	2.00	

ENTREES

Chicken	7.00	Spaghetti &	
Fish	8.00	Meatballs	6.50
Steak	10.00	Vegetable Stew	7.50

DESSERTS

Pie	3.50	Fresh Strawberries	4.00
Cake	3.50		

32. Julia ate at Sammy's Cafe yesterday. She ordered a bowl of vegetable soup and a large salad. How much did she pay?

Ⓐ $3.00. Ⓒ $5.50.
Ⓑ $4.00. Ⓓ $6.00.

33. Ken ordered a small salad, chicken, and rice. How much did he spend?

Ⓐ $11.50. Ⓒ $12.50.
Ⓑ $12.00. Ⓓ $13.00.

34. Sally ate a cup of onion soup, fish, and peas. How much was her bill?

Ⓐ $11.50. Ⓒ $13.00.
Ⓑ $12.50. Ⓓ $12.00.

35. Jeff had a cup of vegetable soup, steak, french fries, and carrots. How much did he spend at the restaurant?

Ⓐ $16.00. Ⓒ $15.00.
Ⓑ $15.50. Ⓓ $14.50.

36. Dora ordered a small salad, vegetable stew, and a piece of cake for dessert. What did she pay?

Ⓐ $11.50. Ⓒ $12.50.
Ⓑ $12.00. Ⓓ $13.00.

37. Ted ordered a bowl of onion soup, chicken, carrots, peas, and fresh strawberries. How much did he pay?

Ⓐ $16.00. Ⓒ $17.00.
Ⓑ $18.00. Ⓓ $17.50.

H LISTENING ASSESSMENT: Ordering a Meal

Read and listen to the questions. Then listen to the conversation and answer the questions.

38. Where is the conversation taking place?

Ⓐ In a supermarket.
Ⓑ In a restaurant.
Ⓒ In a home.
Ⓓ In a school lunchroom.

39. What is the customer going to have for an appetizer?

Ⓐ A glass of milk.
Ⓑ An order of rice.
Ⓒ The baked chicken.
Ⓓ A bowl of soup.

40. How many side orders is the customer going to have?

Ⓐ None.
Ⓑ One.
Ⓒ Two.
Ⓓ Three.

I WRITING ASSESSMENT

What do you usually buy at the supermarket or other food store? How much do you usually spend? Write about it on a separate sheet of paper.

J SPEAKING ASSESSMENT

I can ask and answer these questions:

Ask Answer
☐ ☐ What foods do you like?
☐ ☐ What did you have for breakfast today?
☐ ☐ What did you have for dinner yesterday?

32 Ⓐ Ⓑ Ⓒ Ⓓ   35 Ⓐ Ⓑ Ⓒ Ⓓ   38 Ⓐ Ⓑ Ⓒ Ⓓ
33 Ⓐ Ⓑ Ⓒ Ⓓ   36 Ⓐ Ⓑ Ⓒ Ⓓ   39 Ⓐ Ⓑ Ⓒ Ⓓ
34 Ⓐ Ⓑ Ⓒ Ⓓ   37 Ⓐ Ⓑ Ⓒ Ⓓ   40 Ⓐ Ⓑ Ⓒ Ⓓ

STOP

Name _____

Date _____ Class _____

A SMALL TALK AT WORK & AT SCHOOL

Choose the correct response.

1. What time is the break?
   Ⓐ It's on Friday.
   Ⓑ Every morning.
   Ⓒ It's at 10:30.
   Ⓓ Five days a week.

2. What's the weather forecast for tomorrow?
   Ⓐ It's raining.
   Ⓑ It's going to rain.
   Ⓒ It rained.
   Ⓓ It didn't rain.

3. I'm really tired today.
   Ⓐ Congratulations!
   Ⓑ That's great!
   Ⓒ I'm glad to hear that.
   Ⓓ I'm sorry to hear that.

4. It's very hot in the building today.
   Ⓐ I agree. It's hot.
   Ⓑ I agree. It isn't very hot.
   Ⓒ I disagree. It's hot.
   Ⓓ I disagree. It's very hot.

5. What kind of TV shows do you like?
   Ⓐ You like news programs.
   Ⓑ I like news programs.
   Ⓒ I play baseball.
   Ⓓ I like adventure movies.

6. Did you see the president on TV last night?
   Ⓐ No, he wasn't.
   Ⓑ No, you didn't.
   Ⓒ Yes, I did.
   Ⓓ Yes, you did.

7. Do you think Mr. Lawson will give a math test tomorrow?
   Ⓐ I agree.
   Ⓑ I disagree.
   Ⓒ I think she will.
   Ⓓ I think he will.

8. Do you think it'll rain tomorrow?
   Ⓐ Maybe it will, and maybe it won't.
   Ⓑ Maybe we will, and maybe we won't.
   Ⓒ Maybe you will, and maybe you won't.
   Ⓓ Maybe I will, and maybe I won't.

9. Do you think we'll have to work overtime?
   Ⓐ Maybe we did, and maybe we didn't.
   Ⓑ Maybe we do, and maybe we don't.
   Ⓒ Maybe we will, and maybe we won't.
   Ⓓ Maybe we are, and maybe we aren't.

10. Are you going out for lunch today?
    Ⓐ No. I'm going to a restaurant.
    Ⓑ No. I'm going to eat in my office.
    Ⓒ Yes. I'm going to eat in my office.
    Ⓓ Yes. I'm not going out for lunch.

1 Ⓐ Ⓑ Ⓒ Ⓓ   4 Ⓐ Ⓑ Ⓒ Ⓓ   7 Ⓐ Ⓑ Ⓒ Ⓓ   10 Ⓐ Ⓑ Ⓒ Ⓓ

2 Ⓐ Ⓑ Ⓒ Ⓓ   5 Ⓐ Ⓑ Ⓒ Ⓓ   8 Ⓐ Ⓑ Ⓒ Ⓓ

3 Ⓐ Ⓑ Ⓒ Ⓓ   6 Ⓐ Ⓑ Ⓒ Ⓓ   9 Ⓐ Ⓑ Ⓒ Ⓓ

Go to the next page ⟩   **15**

B GRAMMAR IN CONTEXT: Invitations & Offers

Choose the correct answer to complete the conversations.

11. Would _____ like some milk?
- (A) you'll
- (B) you
- (C) you're
- (D) you do

12. _____ I'd love some.
- (A) Yes. Thanks.
- (B) No. Thanks.
- (C) No thank you.
- (D) Please don't.

13. Would you like to _____ with me after work today?
- (A) will have dinner
- (B) has dinner
- (C) having dinner
- (D) have dinner

14. I'm sorry. _____
- (A) You can't.
- (B) You can.
- (C) I can't.
- (D) I can.

15. _____ you sure?
- (A) Do
- (B) Does
- (C) Is
- (D) Are

16. Yes. _____ work late.
- (A) I have to
- (B) I have
- (C) You have
- (D) I'm

17. _____ like to go sailing with me?
- (A) Did you
- (B) Did I
- (C) Would you
- (D) Would I

18. No, _____.
- (A) I don't
- (B) I don't think so
- (C) I think so
- (D) I think

19. Why _____?
- (A) don't
- (B) doesn't
- (C) no
- (D) not

20. _____ get seasick.
- (A) He might
- (B) I'm
- (C) I'm afraid I might
- (D) You're afraid

. . . .

11 Ⓐ Ⓑ Ⓒ Ⓓ   14 Ⓐ Ⓑ Ⓒ Ⓓ   17 Ⓐ Ⓑ Ⓒ Ⓓ   20 Ⓐ Ⓑ Ⓒ Ⓓ

12 Ⓐ Ⓑ Ⓒ Ⓓ   15 Ⓐ Ⓑ Ⓒ Ⓓ   18 Ⓐ Ⓑ Ⓒ Ⓓ

13 Ⓐ Ⓑ Ⓒ Ⓓ   16 Ⓐ Ⓑ Ⓒ Ⓓ   19 Ⓐ Ⓑ Ⓒ Ⓓ

Go to the next page ➡

C GRAMMAR IN CONTEXT: Asking for Clarification

Choose the correct answer to complete the conversations.

21. Will the train _____ soon?
- Ⓐ will arrive
- Ⓑ arrive
- Ⓒ going to arrive
- Ⓓ is going to arrive

22. Yes. _____ in five minutes.
- Ⓐ Arrive
- Ⓑ Going to arrive
- Ⓒ It arrive
- Ⓓ It'll arrive

23. _____
- Ⓐ In five minutes?
- Ⓑ It'll arrive?
- Ⓒ Yes, it will.
- Ⓓ No?

24. Yes. _____
- Ⓐ It's going to.
- Ⓑ You'll arrive.
- Ⓒ I will.
- Ⓓ That's right.

25. My birthday is _____ May 3rd.
- Ⓐ from
- Ⓑ with
- Ⓒ on
- Ⓓ at

26. May _____?
- Ⓐ who
- Ⓑ what
- Ⓒ why
- Ⓓ how

27. Where _____ you live?
- Ⓐ do
- Ⓑ does
- Ⓒ is
- Ⓓ are

28. I live _____ apartment 3-C.
- Ⓐ on
- Ⓑ with
- Ⓒ for
- Ⓓ in

29. _____ 3-G?
- Ⓐ Did you live
- Ⓑ Do you live
- Ⓒ Did you say
- Ⓓ Do you say

30. _____
- Ⓐ Yes. 3-G.
- Ⓑ Yes. 3-C.
- Ⓒ No. 3-G.
- Ⓓ No. 3-C.

21 Ⓐ Ⓑ Ⓒ Ⓓ   24 Ⓐ Ⓑ Ⓒ Ⓓ   27 Ⓐ Ⓑ Ⓒ Ⓓ   30 Ⓐ Ⓑ Ⓒ Ⓓ

22 Ⓐ Ⓑ Ⓒ Ⓓ   25 Ⓐ Ⓑ Ⓒ Ⓓ   28 Ⓐ Ⓑ Ⓒ Ⓓ

23 Ⓐ Ⓑ Ⓒ Ⓓ   26 Ⓐ Ⓑ Ⓒ Ⓓ   29 Ⓐ Ⓑ Ⓒ Ⓓ

Go to the next page ⟶   **17** 🔴

D CLOZE READING: Small Talk at Work

Choose the correct answers to complete the story.

"Small talk" [of / at / when]³¹ work is very important. Co-workers [talk / talks / talking]³¹ with

each other about many different things. They talk about [my / your / their]³² favorite movies and

TV programs. They talk [above / about / with]³³ music and sports. [Much / Many / Co-workers]³⁴

people also talk about the weather. Some subjects [don't / aren't / isn't]³⁵ very good for "small talk"

in some countries, but in other countries [this / that / these]³⁶ subjects are very common.

For example, questions about a person's salary or the [price / receipt / how much]³⁷ of a person's

home are common in some countries but very unusual in other countries.

E LISTENING ASSESSMENT: An Invitation

Read and listen to the questions. Then listen to the conversation and answer the questions.

38. What day is it?
- Ⓐ Tuesday.
- Ⓑ Wednesday.
- Ⓒ Thursday.
- Ⓓ We don't know.

39. What are they going to do tomorrow?
- Ⓐ Make dinner.
- Ⓑ Have dinner.
- Ⓒ Go to a class.
- Ⓓ Go to a meeting.

40. Where are they going to meet?
- Ⓐ At the restaurant.
- Ⓑ At the computer class.
- Ⓒ On Wednesday.
- Ⓓ At the person's office.

F WRITING ASSESSMENT

Describe your plans for the weekend. What are you going to do? What might you do? Write about it on a separate sheet of paper.

G SPEAKING ASSESSMENT

I can ask and answer these questions:

Ask Answer
- ☐ ☐ How do you like the weather today?
- ☐ ☐ What's the weather forecast for tomorrow?
- ☐ ☐ What kind of TV shows do you like?
- ☐ ☐ What kind of music do you like?
- ☐ ☐ What did you do last weekend?
- ☐ ☐ What are you going to do next weekend?

31 Ⓐ Ⓑ Ⓒ Ⓓ   34 Ⓐ Ⓑ Ⓒ Ⓓ   37 Ⓐ Ⓑ Ⓒ Ⓓ   40 Ⓐ Ⓑ Ⓒ Ⓓ

32 Ⓐ Ⓑ Ⓒ Ⓓ   35 Ⓐ Ⓑ Ⓒ Ⓓ   38 Ⓐ Ⓑ Ⓒ Ⓓ

33 Ⓐ Ⓑ Ⓒ Ⓓ   36 Ⓐ Ⓑ Ⓒ Ⓓ   39 Ⓐ Ⓑ Ⓒ Ⓓ

A   SMALL TALK AT WORK & AT SCHOOL

Choose the correct response.

1. How do you like our new boss?
   I think she's _____ our old boss.
   - Ⓐ friendly
   - Ⓑ friendlier
   - Ⓒ friendlier than
   - Ⓓ more friendly

2. What do you think about our new English teacher?
   I think he's _____ our old teacher.
   - Ⓐ nicer
   - Ⓑ nicer than
   - Ⓒ more nice than
   - Ⓓ more nice

3. What's your favorite kind of music?
   Rock music. I think it's _____ other kinds of music.
   - Ⓐ better than
   - Ⓑ good than
   - Ⓒ more good than
   - Ⓓ more better than

4. The weather today is beautiful.
   I agree. It's _____ yesterday.
   - Ⓐ nice
   - Ⓑ nicer
   - Ⓒ nicer than
   - Ⓓ more nice than

5. I think your computer is newer than mine.
   It is. Mine is newer than _____.
   - Ⓐ my
   - Ⓑ mine
   - Ⓒ your
   - Ⓓ yours

6. Our math class isn't very interesting any more.
   I agree. It _____ more interesting.
   - Ⓐ to be used
   - Ⓑ used to be
   - Ⓒ used be to
   - Ⓓ was to be

7. Should I work overtime today or tomorrow?
   _____ work overtime today.
   - Ⓐ You think I should
   - Ⓑ You should I think
   - Ⓒ I think you should
   - Ⓓ I should you think

8. My locker isn't as clean as your locker.
   You're right. Mine _____ yours.
   - Ⓐ is cleaner than
   - Ⓑ isn't cleaner than
   - Ⓒ is as clean as
   - Ⓓ isn't as clean as

9. You know, the food in the cafeteria isn't as good as it used to be.
   I agree. The food _____.
   - Ⓐ is better now
   - Ⓑ are better now
   - Ⓒ used to be
   - Ⓓ used to be better

10. I think our science class is more interesting than our history class.
    I disagree. I think history _____ science.
    - Ⓐ isn't as interesting
    - Ⓑ isn't as interesting as
    - Ⓒ is more interesting
    - Ⓓ is more interesting than

· ·

1 Ⓐ Ⓑ Ⓒ Ⓓ   4 Ⓐ Ⓑ Ⓒ Ⓓ   7 Ⓐ Ⓑ Ⓒ Ⓓ   10 Ⓐ Ⓑ Ⓒ Ⓓ

2 Ⓐ Ⓑ Ⓒ Ⓓ   5 Ⓐ Ⓑ Ⓒ Ⓓ   8 Ⓐ Ⓑ Ⓒ Ⓓ

3 Ⓐ Ⓑ Ⓒ Ⓓ   6 Ⓐ Ⓑ Ⓒ Ⓓ   9 Ⓐ Ⓑ Ⓒ Ⓓ   **Go to the next page** ⟩   **19**

B GRAMMAR IN CONTEXT: Compliments

Choose the correct answer to complete the conversations.

11. _____ a very nice bicycle.
- Ⓐ That
- Ⓑ That's
- Ⓒ This
- Ⓓ These

12. _____
- Ⓐ It is that.
- Ⓑ It's a bicycle.
- Ⓒ Thanks.
- Ⓓ You're welcome.

13. _____ fast?
- Ⓐ Is it
- Ⓑ It is
- Ⓒ Are they
- Ⓓ They are

14. Yes. It's _____ my old bicycle.
- Ⓐ faster
- Ⓑ faster than
- Ⓒ more fast
- Ⓓ more

15. These cookies _____.
- Ⓐ is delicious
- Ⓑ more delicious
- Ⓒ much more delicious
- Ⓓ are delicious

16. Thanks. My new recipe is _____ my old one.
- Ⓐ much better than
- Ⓑ much better
- Ⓒ more good
- Ⓓ better

17. Your apartment _____.
- Ⓐ nicer than
- Ⓑ is nicer than
- Ⓒ is very nice
- Ⓓ are very nice

18. Thank you. Do you like _____?
- Ⓐ my sofa is new
- Ⓑ my sofa is newer
- Ⓒ my new sofa
- Ⓓ newer sofa

19. Yes. It's _____ than your old one.
- Ⓐ attractive
- Ⓑ more attractive
- Ⓒ much attractive
- Ⓓ much more

20. I think so, too. It's also _____ comfortable.
- Ⓐ much
- Ⓑ good
- Ⓒ better
- Ⓓ more

11 Ⓐ Ⓑ Ⓒ Ⓓ 14 Ⓐ Ⓑ Ⓒ Ⓓ 17 Ⓐ Ⓑ Ⓒ Ⓓ 20 Ⓐ Ⓑ Ⓒ Ⓓ

12 Ⓐ Ⓑ Ⓒ Ⓓ 15 Ⓐ Ⓑ Ⓒ Ⓓ 18 Ⓐ Ⓑ Ⓒ Ⓓ

13 Ⓐ Ⓑ Ⓒ Ⓓ 16 Ⓐ Ⓑ Ⓒ Ⓓ 19 Ⓐ Ⓑ Ⓒ Ⓓ Go to the next page ➡

C **GRAMMAR IN CONTEXT: Appropriate Language in Social Situations**

Choose the correct answer to complete the conversations.

21. _____ You're stepping on my foot.
- (A) Excuse me.
- (B) Excuse.
- (C) You excuse me.
- (D) I excuse you.

22. Oh. _____
- (A) You apologize.
- (B) I apologize.
- (C) You're apologizing.
- (D) I'm apologizing.

23. That's okay. _____
- (A) Think.
- (B) Don't think.
- (C) Worry about it.
- (D) Don't worry about it.

24. _____
- (A) It's very sorry.
- (B) We're very sorry.
- (C) I'm really sorry.
- (D) You're really sorry.

25. You _____. Is something wrong?
- (A) are looking
- (B) look sad
- (C) sad
- (D) the matter

26. Yes. I have _____.
- (A) some bad news
- (B) some bad
- (C) some good news
- (D) some good

27. What _____?
- (A) happen
- (B) happened
- (C) happening
- (D) going to happen

28. My husband _____ yesterday.
- (A) lose job
- (B) lost job
- (C) lose his job
- (D) lost his job

29. I'm _____ that.
- (A) sorry
- (B) sorry to
- (C) sorry to hear
- (D) sorry hear

30. _____
- (A) Thank you.
- (B) I agree.
- (C) I disagree.
- (D) You're sorry.

21 (A) (B) (C) (D)   24 (A) (B) (C) (D)   27 (A) (B) (C) (D)   30 (A) (B) (C) (D)

22 (A) (B) (C) (D)   25 (A) (B) (C) (D)   28 (A) (B) (C) (D)

23 (A) (B) (C) (D)   26 (A) (B) (C) (D)   29 (A) (B) (C) (D)   **Go to the next page** ⟹

D CLOZE READING: A Thank-You Note

Choose the correct answers to complete the note.

Dear Alan,

Thank you [with (A) | for (●) | by (C)] the wonderful dinner yesterday. [They (A) | It (B) | I (C)] [31] was

delicious. The vegetable soup [were (A) | was (B) | did (C)] [32] great, the hamburgers [were (A) | was (B) | are (C)] [33]

excellent, and the [potatoes (A) | carrots (B) | chili (C)] [34] was also very good. In fact, I think your recipe

is much [good (A) | more good (B) | better (C)] [35] than [my (A) | mine (B) | me (C)] [36].

Thank you again. Next time [I'll (A) | I'm (B) | I (C)] [37] invite you to MY place for dinner.

Sincerely,

Natalie

E LISTENING ASSESSMENT: Expressing Opinions

Read and listen to the questions. Then listen to the conversation and answer the questions.

38. What do they disagree about?
   - Ⓐ The buildings.
   - Ⓑ The streets.
   - Ⓒ The people.
   - Ⓓ The weather.

39. What do they agree about?
   - Ⓐ The people and the buildings.
   - Ⓑ The buildings and the parks.
   - Ⓒ The streets and the buildings.
   - Ⓓ The streets and the people.

40. Which opinion do they probably agree about?
   - Ⓐ The buildings in other cities are more interesting.
   - Ⓑ The people in other cities are friendlier.
   - Ⓒ The streets in other cities are cleaner.
   - Ⓓ The parks in other cities are more beautiful.

F WRITING ASSESSMENT

Compare two different places you know. Write about the streets, the buildings, the weather, the people, and life in these two places. (Use a separate sheet of paper.)

G SPEAKING ASSESSMENT

I can ask and answer these questions:

Ask Answer
- ☐ ☐ What's your favorite food?
- ☐ ☐ How do you like my new _____?
- ☐ ☐ What do you think about our English class?
- ☐ ☐ What's your opinion about life in our city?

. . . .

31 Ⓐ Ⓑ Ⓒ Ⓓ   34 Ⓐ Ⓑ Ⓒ Ⓓ   37 Ⓐ Ⓑ Ⓒ Ⓓ   40 Ⓐ Ⓑ Ⓒ Ⓓ

32 Ⓐ Ⓑ Ⓒ Ⓓ   35 Ⓐ Ⓑ Ⓒ Ⓓ   38 Ⓐ Ⓑ Ⓒ Ⓓ

33 Ⓐ Ⓑ Ⓒ Ⓓ   36 Ⓐ Ⓑ Ⓒ Ⓓ   39 Ⓐ Ⓑ Ⓒ Ⓓ

 22

Name _____

Date _____ Class _____

A SHOPPING REQUESTS & LOCATING ITEMS

These people are shopping in a department store. Where is each person shopping?
Choose the correct department.

Ex: "I'm looking for a new TV."
- Ⓐ Appliances
- ● Home Entertainment
- Ⓑ Jewelry
- Ⓓ Customer Service

1. "Do you have this tie in blue?"
   - Ⓐ Jewelry
   - Ⓒ Men's Clothing
   - Ⓑ Furniture
   - Ⓓ Women's Clothing

2. "Is this dishwasher the best one you have?"
   - Ⓐ Furniture
   - Ⓒ Customer Service
   - Ⓑ Appliances
   - Ⓓ Home Entertainment

3. "I want to buy a ring."
   - Ⓐ Jewelry
   - Ⓒ Home Entertainment
   - Ⓑ Furniture
   - Ⓓ Appliances

4. "We need a new kitchen table."
   - Ⓐ Furniture
   - Ⓒ Cosmetics
   - Ⓑ Jewelry
   - Ⓓ Appliances

5. "Do you have any longer dresses?"
   - Ⓐ Jewelry
   - Ⓒ Women's Clothing
   - Ⓑ Furniture
   - Ⓓ Home Entertainment

6. "I want to return this item."
   - Ⓐ Rest Rooms
   - Ⓒ Appliances
   - Ⓑ Cosmetics
   - Ⓓ Customer Service

7. "I'm looking for a shirt for my little boy."
   - Ⓐ Toys
   - Ⓒ Men's Clothing
   - Ⓑ Appliances
   - Ⓓ Children's Clothing

B UNDERSTANDING ATM INSTRUCTIONS

Read the ATM instruction. Choose the correct answer.

8. Enter the amount in dollars and cents.
   - Ⓐ OKAY
   - Ⓑ 4761
   - Ⓒ $50.00
   - Ⓓ ENTER

9. Choose a transaction: WITHDRAWAL
   - Ⓐ Insert card.
   - Ⓑ Get money.
   - Ⓒ Put in money.
   - Ⓓ Press ENTER.

10. Choose a transaction: DEPOSIT
    - Ⓐ Put in money.
    - Ⓑ Press OKAY.
    - Ⓒ Get money.
    - Ⓓ Insert card.

11. Enter your PIN (Personal Identification Number)
    - Ⓐ $0.00
    - Ⓑ $50.00
    - Ⓒ 4761
    - Ⓓ P-I-N

12. Balance Inquiry
    - Ⓐ Choose another account.
    - Ⓑ Last Deposit: $463.12
    - Ⓒ Last Withdrawal: $100.00
    - Ⓓ Funds available: $1,241.63

13. Do you want to make another transaction?
    - Ⓐ Enter your PIN.
    - Ⓑ Press YES or NO.
    - Ⓒ Enter the amount.
    - Ⓓ Insert your card.

1 Ⓐ Ⓑ Ⓒ Ⓓ   5 Ⓐ Ⓑ Ⓒ Ⓓ   9 Ⓐ Ⓑ Ⓒ Ⓓ   13 Ⓐ Ⓑ Ⓒ Ⓓ

2 Ⓐ Ⓑ Ⓒ Ⓓ   6 Ⓐ Ⓑ Ⓒ Ⓓ   10 Ⓐ Ⓑ Ⓒ Ⓓ

3 Ⓐ Ⓑ Ⓒ Ⓓ   7 Ⓐ Ⓑ Ⓒ Ⓓ   11 Ⓐ Ⓑ Ⓒ Ⓓ

4 Ⓐ Ⓑ Ⓒ Ⓓ   8 Ⓐ Ⓑ Ⓒ Ⓓ   12 Ⓐ Ⓑ Ⓒ Ⓓ

Go to the next page ⟹

C INTERPRETING A CHECK

	1024
	(1) _____
Pay to the order of (2) _____	$ (3) _____
(4) _____ Dollars	
For (5) _____	(6) _____

057009345 200042534 1024

Look at the information. Where should you write it? Choose the correct line on the check.

14. Savemax Clothing Store
- Ⓐ Line 2
- Ⓑ Line 4
- Ⓒ Line 5
- Ⓓ Line 6

15. 36.40
- Ⓐ Line 1
- Ⓑ Line 3
- Ⓒ Line 4
- Ⓓ Line 6

16. Nov. 22, 2018
- Ⓐ Line 1
- Ⓑ Line 3
- Ⓒ Line 5
- Ⓓ Line 6

17. pants & belt
- Ⓐ Line 2
- Ⓑ Line 4
- Ⓒ Line 5
- Ⓓ Line 6

18. *Pedro Martinez*
- Ⓐ Line 3
- Ⓑ Line 4
- Ⓒ Line 5
- Ⓓ Line 6

19. Thirty-six and 40/100.................................
- Ⓐ Line 2
- Ⓑ Line 3
- Ⓒ Line 4
- Ⓓ Line 5

D GRAMMAR IN CONTEXT: Problems with Purchases; Returning an Item

Ex: _____ help you?
- Ⓐ Can you
- Ⓑ You can
- ● May I
- Ⓓ I may

20. Yes. _____ return this DVD player.
- Ⓐ I want
- Ⓑ I want to
- Ⓒ You want
- Ⓓ You want to

21. Is there a _____ with it?
- Ⓐ problem
- Ⓑ matter
- Ⓒ wrong
- Ⓓ something

22. Yes. It's _____. It doesn't work.
- Ⓐ a DVD player
- Ⓑ wrong
- Ⓒ the matter
- Ⓓ broken

23. Do you have your _____?
- Ⓐ DVD player
- Ⓑ check
- Ⓒ receipt
- Ⓓ ATM card

24. Yes. _____
- Ⓐ Here I am.
- Ⓑ Here they are.
- Ⓒ I don't have it.
- Ⓓ Here it is.

14 Ⓐ Ⓑ Ⓒ Ⓓ   17 Ⓐ Ⓑ Ⓒ Ⓓ   20 Ⓐ Ⓑ Ⓒ Ⓓ   23 Ⓐ Ⓑ Ⓒ Ⓓ

15 Ⓐ Ⓑ Ⓒ Ⓓ   18 Ⓐ Ⓑ Ⓒ Ⓓ   21 Ⓐ Ⓑ Ⓒ Ⓓ   24 Ⓐ Ⓑ Ⓒ Ⓓ

16 Ⓐ Ⓑ Ⓒ Ⓓ   19 Ⓐ Ⓑ Ⓒ Ⓓ   22 Ⓐ Ⓑ Ⓒ Ⓓ   **Go to the next page** ⟶

E GRAMMAR IN CONTEXT: Problems with Purchases; Exchanging an Item

25. I'd like to _____ this cell phone.
- Ⓐ give
- Ⓑ return
- Ⓒ take
- Ⓓ call

26. What's the _____ with it?
- Ⓐ matter
- Ⓑ wrong
- Ⓒ why
- Ⓓ what's wrong

27. _____ small enough.
- Ⓐ They aren't
- Ⓑ Aren't they
- Ⓒ It isn't
- Ⓓ Isn't it

28. Do you want to _____ it for a smaller one?
- Ⓐ return
- Ⓑ buy
- Ⓒ give
- Ⓓ exchange

29. _____ a smaller one?
- Ⓐ You do have
- Ⓑ Do you have
- Ⓒ Have you
- Ⓓ You do

30. Yes. This used to be the _____ one, but now we have a smaller one.
- Ⓐ smallest
- Ⓑ more small
- Ⓒ more smallest
- Ⓓ much small

31. Then I think _____ exchange it.
- Ⓐ I like
- Ⓑ you like
- Ⓒ you'd like to
- Ⓓ I'd like to

32. Okay. Go to the Electronics _____. Somebody there will help you.
- Ⓐ store
- Ⓑ furniture
- Ⓒ department
- Ⓓ entertainment

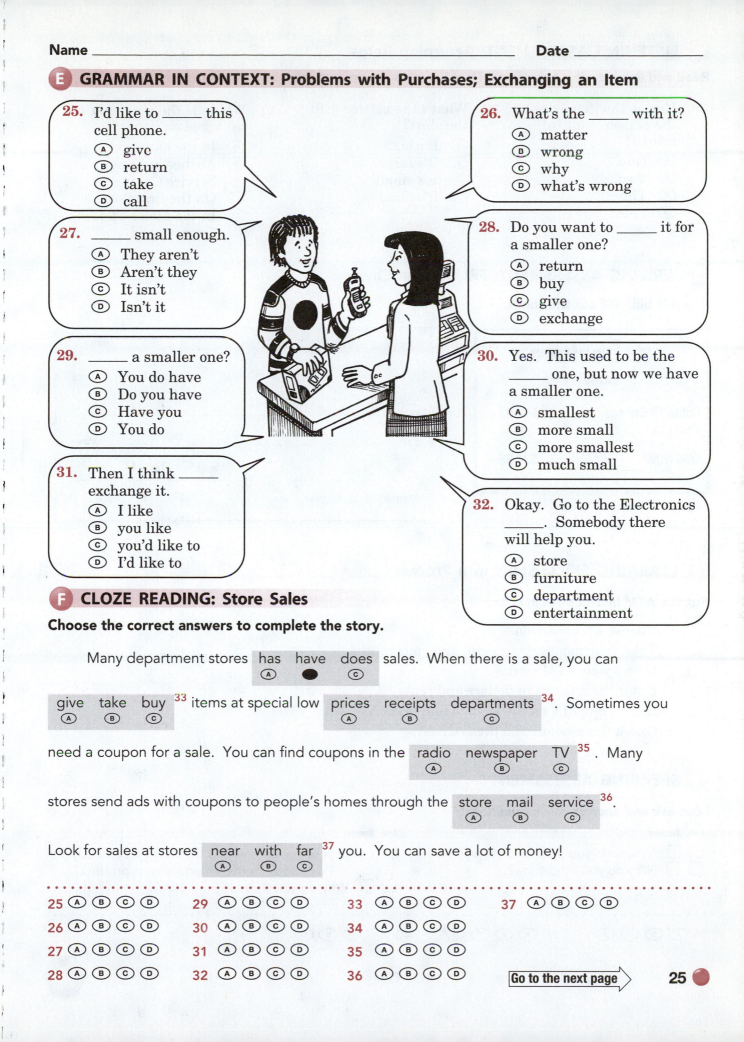

F CLOZE READING: Store Sales

Choose the correct answers to complete the story.

Many department stores [has Ⓐ **have ●** does Ⓒ] sales. When there is a sale, you can

[give Ⓐ take Ⓑ buy Ⓒ] ³³ items at special low [prices Ⓐ receipts Ⓑ departments Ⓒ] ³⁴. Sometimes you

need a coupon for a sale. You can find coupons in the [radio Ⓐ newspaper Ⓑ TV Ⓒ] ³⁵. Many

stores send ads with coupons to people's homes through the [store Ⓐ mail Ⓑ service Ⓒ] ³⁶.

Look for sales at stores [near Ⓐ with Ⓑ far Ⓒ] ³⁷ you. You can save a lot of money!

- -

25 Ⓐ Ⓑ Ⓒ Ⓓ	29 Ⓐ Ⓑ Ⓒ Ⓓ	33 Ⓐ Ⓑ Ⓒ Ⓓ	37 Ⓐ Ⓑ Ⓒ Ⓓ
26 Ⓐ Ⓑ Ⓒ Ⓓ	30 Ⓐ Ⓑ Ⓒ Ⓓ	34 Ⓐ Ⓑ Ⓒ Ⓓ	
27 Ⓐ Ⓑ Ⓒ Ⓓ	31 Ⓐ Ⓑ Ⓒ Ⓓ	35 Ⓐ Ⓑ Ⓒ Ⓓ	
28 Ⓐ Ⓑ Ⓒ Ⓓ	32 Ⓐ Ⓑ Ⓒ Ⓓ	36 Ⓐ Ⓑ Ⓒ Ⓓ	

Go to the next page ⟹

G LISTENING ASSESSMENT: Returning Items

Read and listen to the questions. Then listen to the conversation and answer the questions.

38. How many items does the person want to return?
- (A) One.
- (B) Two.
- (C) Three.
- (D) Four.

39. What's the matter with the shirt?
- (A) It's big.
- (B) It's large.
- (C) It's small.
- (D) It's blue.

40. Where is the conversation taking place?
- (A) In the elevator.
- (B) At the Customer Service Counter.
- (C) On the first floor.
- (D) In the Men's Clothing Department.

H WRITING ASSESSMENT: Fill Out the Check

Pay this bill. Fill out the check.

Metrovision
Cable TV

Cable TV Service	$24.95
Past Due	0.00
DUE NOW	**$24.95**

1024

Pay to the order of _____ $_____

_____ Dollars

For _____   _____

057009345 200042534 1024

I LEARNING SKILL: Steps in a Process

Put the ATM instructions in order.

_____ Choose a transaction.

_____ Take your money, your card, and your receipt.

___1___ Insert your ATM card.

_____ Enter the amount in dollars and cents.

_____ Enter your PIN on the keypad and press ENTER.

_____ Check the amount and press OKAY.

J SPEAKING ASSESSMENT

I can ask and answer these questions:

Ask Answer
☐ ☐ Where do you shop for clothing?
☐ ☐ Why do you shop there?

Ask Answer
☐ ☐ In your opinion, what's the best place to buy a TV or other home entertainment product?
☐ ☐ Why do you think so?

38 (A) (B) (C) (D)   39 (A) (B) (C) (D)   40 (A) (B) (C) (D)

 STOP

Name _____

Date _____ Class _____

7

A SCHEDULES

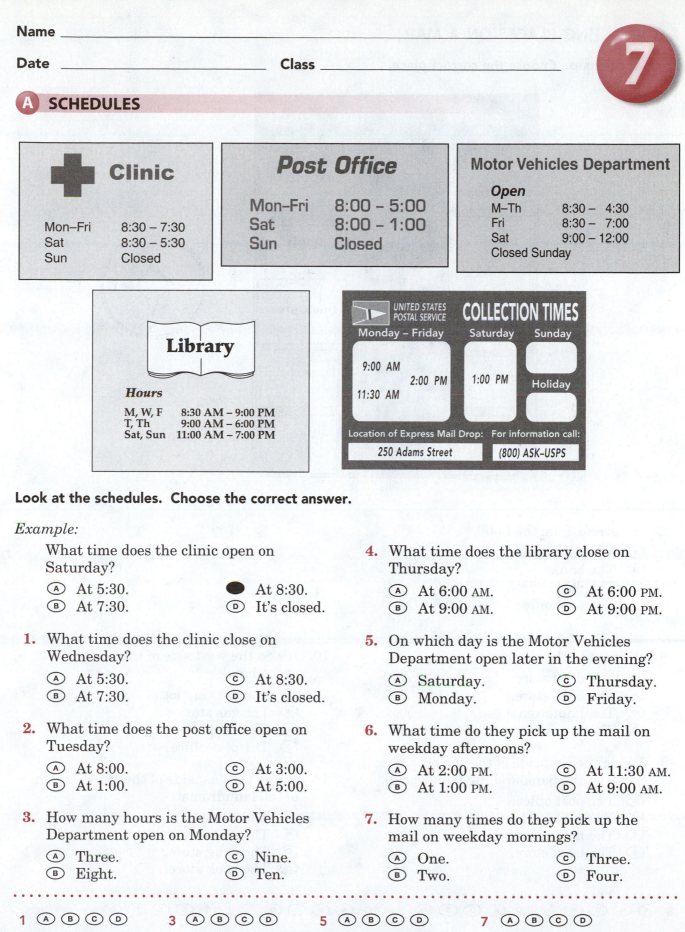

Clinic

Mon–Fri	8:30 – 7:30
Sat	8:30 – 5:30
Sun	Closed

Post Office

Mon–Fri	8:00 – 5:00
Sat	8:00 – 1:00
Sun	Closed

Motor Vehicles Department

Open

M–Th	8:30 – 4:30
Fri	8:30 – 7:00
Sat	9:00 – 12:00
Closed Sunday	

Library

Hours

M, W, F	8:30 AM – 9:00 PM
T, Th	9:00 AM – 6:00 PM
Sat, Sun	11:00 AM – 7:00 PM

UNITED STATES POSTAL SERVICE — **COLLECTION TIMES**

| Monday – Friday | Saturday | Sunday |
| 9:00 AM 2:00 PM 11:30 AM | 1:00 PM | Holiday |

| Location of Express Mail Drop: | For information call: |
| 250 Adams Street | (800) ASK-USPS |

Look at the schedules. Choose the correct answer.

Example:

What time does the clinic open on Saturday?
- (A) At 5:30.
- (B) At 7:30.
- ● At 8:30.
- (D) It's closed.

1. What time does the clinic close on Wednesday?
- (A) At 5:30.
- (C) At 8:30.
- (B) At 7:30.
- (D) It's closed.

2. What time does the post office open on Tuesday?
- (A) At 8:00.
- (C) At 3:00.
- (B) At 1:00.
- (D) At 5:00.

3. How many hours is the Motor Vehicles Department open on Monday?
- (A) Three.
- (C) Nine.
- (B) Eight.
- (D) Ten.

4. What time does the library close on Thursday?
- (A) At 6:00 AM.
- (C) At 6:00 PM.
- (B) At 9:00 AM.
- (D) At 9:00 PM.

5. On which day is the Motor Vehicles Department open later in the evening?
- (A) Saturday.
- (C) Thursday.
- (B) Monday.
- (D) Friday.

6. What time do they pick up the mail on weekday afternoons?
- (A) At 2:00 PM.
- (C) At 11:30 AM.
- (B) At 1:00 PM.
- (D) At 9:00 AM.

7. How many times do they pick up the mail on weekday mornings?
- (A) One.
- (C) Three.
- (B) Two.
- (D) Four.

1 (A) (B) (C) (D)   3 (A) (B) (C) (D)   5 (A) (B) (C) (D)   7 (A) (B) (C) (D)

2 (A) (B) (C) (D)   4 (A) (B) (C) (D)   6 (A) (B) (C) (D)

B   LOCATING PLACES ON A MAP

Look at the map. Choose the correct place.

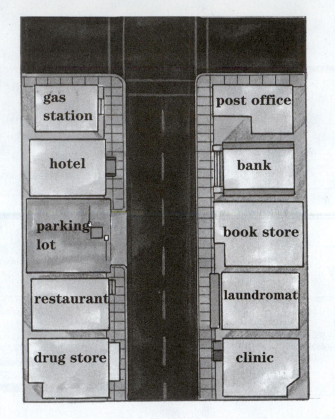

Example:

It's across from the hotel.
- (A) The gas station.
- (B) The bank.
- (C) The parking lot.
- (D) The post office.   (A) ● (C) (D)

8. It's next to the clinic.
- (A) The drug store.
- (B) The book store.
- (C) The laundromat.
- (D) The restaurant.

9. It's on the east side of the street, between the bank and the laundromat.
- (A) The post office.
- (B) The parking lot.
- (C) The hotel.
- (D) The book store.

10. It's on the west side of the street, north of the hotel.
- (A) The parking lot.
- (B) The gas station.
- (C) The bank.
- (D) The post office.

11. It's on the east side of the street, south of the laundromat.
- (A) The clinic.
- (B) The restaurant.
- (C) The drug store.
- (D) The book store.

. . . .

8 (A) (B) (C) (D)   9 (A) (B) (C) (D)   10 (A) (B) (C) (D)   11 (A) (B) (C) (D)

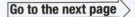

Go to the next page ⟹

C READING: A Bus Schedule

Look at the bus schedule.
Choose the correct answer.

Example:

Where does this bus route start?
- Ⓐ Russell Avenue.
- Ⓑ Metro Plaza.
- Ⓒ Custis Drive.
- Ⓓ King Street.   Ⓐ Ⓑ Ⓒ ⬤

12. Where does this bus route end?
- Ⓐ King Street.
- Ⓑ Braddock Road.
- Ⓒ Russell Avenue.
- Ⓓ Metro Plaza.

13. What time does the first bus leave King Street?
- Ⓐ 5:40 AM.
- Ⓑ 6:13 AM.
- Ⓒ 6:50 PM.
- Ⓓ 7:23 PM.

14. What time does the last bus arrive at Custis Drive?
- Ⓐ 6:06 AM.
- Ⓑ 6:13 AM.
- Ⓒ 7:16 PM.
- Ⓓ 7:23 PM.

15. When does the 7:00 AM bus arrive at Russell Avenue?
- Ⓐ 7:00 AM.
- Ⓑ 7:11 AM.
- Ⓒ 7:11 PM.
- Ⓓ 7:21 AM.

16. Which bus doesn't stop at Metro Plaza?
- Ⓐ The 6:00 AM bus from King Street.
- Ⓑ The 9:00 AM bus from King Street.
- Ⓒ The 1:05 PM bus from King Street.
- Ⓓ The 3:05 PM bus from King Street.

17. How long does it take any bus to go from King Street to Metro Plaza?
- Ⓐ 11 minutes.
- Ⓑ 12 minutes.
- Ⓒ 30 minutes.
- Ⓓ 33 minutes.

18. It's 12:30 PM, and you're at the bus stop on King Street. How long do you have to wait for the bus?
- Ⓐ 1 hour.
- Ⓑ 35 minutes.
- Ⓒ 30 minutes.
- Ⓓ 5 minutes.

Route 18A

King Street	Braddock Road	Russell Avenue	Custis Drive	Metro Plaza
Weekdays				
5:40 AM	5:51	6:01	6:06	6:13
6:00	6:11	6:21	6:26	6:33
6:20	6:31	6:41	6:46	6:53
6:40	6:51	7:01	7:06	7:13
7:00	7:11	7:21	7:26	7:33
7:20	7:31	7:41	7:46	7:53
7:40	7:51	8:01	8:06	8:13
8:00	8:11	8:21	8:26	8:33
8:20	8:31	8:41	8:46	8:53
8:40	8:51	9:01	9:06	9:13
9:00	9:11	9:21	9:26	9:33
10:05	10:15	10:25	10:30	-
11:05	11:15	11:25	11:30	-
12:05 PM	12:15	12:25	12:30	-
1:05	1:15	1:25	1:30	-
2:05	2:15	2:25	2:30	-
3:05	3:16	3:26	3:31	3:38
3:50	4:01	4:11	4:16	4:23
4:10	4:21	4:31	4:36	4:43
4:30	4:41	4:51	4:56	5:03
4:50	5:01	5:11	5:16	5:23
5:10	5:21	5:31	5:36	5:43
5:30	5:41	5:51	5:56	6:03
5:50	6:01	6:11	6:16	6:23
6:10	6:21	6:31	6:36	6:43
6:30	6:41	6:51	6:56	7:03
6:50	7:01	7:11	7:16	7:23

Choose the correct sign.

A

B

C

D

Example:

There are train tracks ahead. Watch out for trains.

Ⓐ Ⓑ ● Ⓓ

19. No left turn.

Ⓐ Ⓑ Ⓒ Ⓓ

20. There's a crosswalk ahead. Watch out for pedestrians.

Ⓐ Ⓑ Ⓒ Ⓓ

21. When you enter this road, let the other cars already on the road go first.

Ⓐ Ⓑ Ⓒ Ⓓ

E **POLICE COMMANDS & TRAFFIC SIGNS**

Choose the correct sign.

A

B

C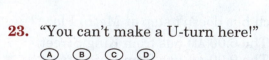

D

Example:

"Stop! You can't enter this street from here!"

Ⓐ Ⓑ Ⓒ ●

22. "Slow down! You're in a school zone!"

Ⓐ Ⓑ Ⓒ Ⓓ

23. "You can't make a U-turn here!"

Ⓐ Ⓑ Ⓒ Ⓓ

24. "Turn around! You're going in the wrong direction!"

Ⓐ Ⓑ Ⓒ Ⓓ

. . . .

19 Ⓐ Ⓑ Ⓒ Ⓓ   **21** Ⓐ Ⓑ Ⓒ Ⓓ   **23** Ⓐ Ⓑ Ⓒ Ⓓ

F GRAMMAR IN CONTEXT: Postal Services

Example:

I want to send this _____ to Texas.

Ⓐ postcard
● package
Ⓒ letter
Ⓓ envelope

25. Do you want to send it _____ surface mail or air mail?

Ⓐ for
Ⓑ with
Ⓒ by
Ⓓ from

26. _____ recommend?

Ⓐ What does it
Ⓑ What do I
Ⓒ What does he
Ⓓ What do you

27. Let's see. It weighs eight _____ and eleven ounces.

Ⓐ inches
Ⓑ pounds
Ⓒ feet
Ⓓ miles

28. How much will it _____?

Ⓐ cost
Ⓑ costs
Ⓒ send
Ⓓ sends

29. _____ $4.50 surface mail or $7.25 air mail.

Ⓐ I'll cost
Ⓑ You'll cost
Ⓒ It'll cost
Ⓓ They'll cost

30. _____ will it take to get there by surface mail?

Ⓐ How much
Ⓑ How many
Ⓒ How short
Ⓓ How long

31. About ten _____.

Ⓐ miles
Ⓑ ounces
Ⓒ days
Ⓓ feet

All right.

32. I think I'll send it by surface mail. And I'd also like a book of first-class _____, please.

Ⓐ postcards
Ⓑ stamps
Ⓒ money orders
Ⓓ aerogrammes

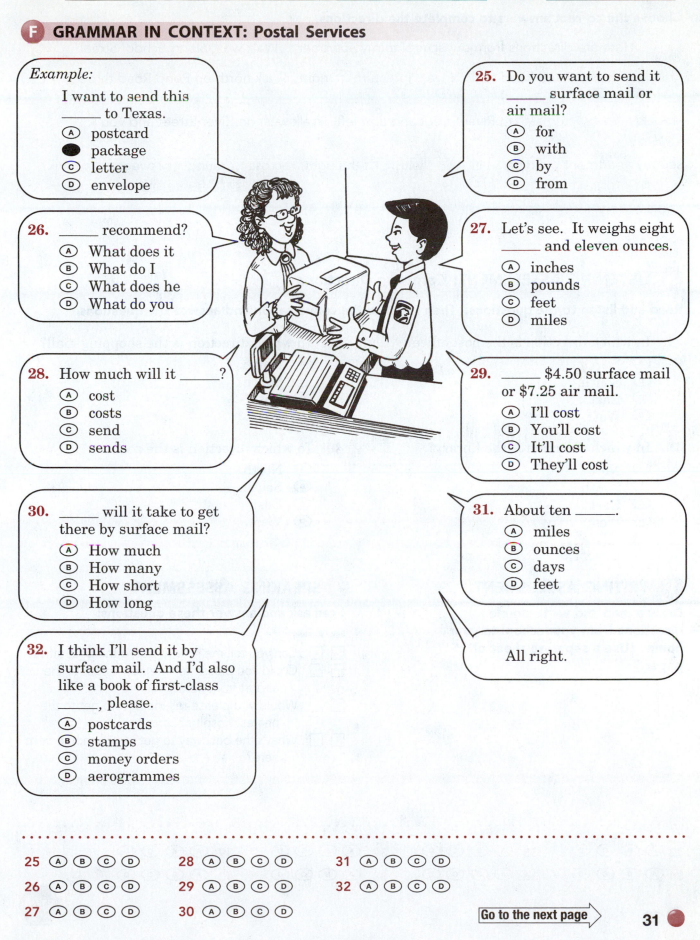

25 Ⓐ Ⓑ Ⓒ Ⓓ   28 Ⓐ Ⓑ Ⓒ Ⓓ   31 Ⓐ Ⓑ Ⓒ Ⓓ

26 Ⓐ Ⓑ Ⓒ Ⓓ   29 Ⓐ Ⓑ Ⓒ Ⓓ   32 Ⓐ Ⓑ Ⓒ Ⓓ

27 Ⓐ Ⓑ Ⓒ Ⓓ   30 Ⓐ Ⓑ Ⓒ Ⓓ

Go to the next page ⟹

G CLOZE READING: Simple Written Directions

Choose the correct answers to complete the directions.

Here are directions from our school to my apartment. Walk west along School Street

for	to	next
Ⓐ	●	Ⓒ

Pond Road and

drive	for	turn
Ⓐ	Ⓑ	Ⓒ

³³ right. Walk north on Pond Road three

blocks	walks	turns
Ⓐ	Ⓑ	Ⓒ

³⁴ to River Street and turn left. Walk west on River Street and you'll

see my apartment building

in	on	with
Ⓐ	Ⓑ	Ⓒ

³⁵ the right,

across	around	between
Ⓐ	Ⓑ	Ⓒ

³⁶ a bank

and a bakery.

H LISTENING ASSESSMENT: Compass Directions

Read and listen to the questions. Then listen to the conversation and answer the questions.

37. In which direction is the post office?
- Ⓐ North.
- Ⓑ South.
- Ⓒ East.
- Ⓓ West.

38. In which direction is the library?
- Ⓐ North.
- Ⓑ South.
- Ⓒ East.
- Ⓓ West.

39. In which direction is the shopping mall?
- Ⓐ North.
- Ⓑ South.
- Ⓒ East.
- Ⓓ West.

40. In which direction is the zoo?
- Ⓐ North.
- Ⓑ South.
- Ⓒ East.
- Ⓓ West.

I WRITING ASSESSMENT

Draw a map and write simple directions from your school to your home. (Use a separate sheet of paper.)

J SPEAKING ASSESSMENT

I can ask and answer these questions:

Ask Answer

☐ ☐ Can you tell me how to get to the post office?

☐ ☐ Could you please tell me how to get to the airport from here?

☐ ☐ Would you please tell me how to get to the nearest hospital?

☐ ☐ What's the best way to get to your home from here?

. . . .

33 Ⓐ Ⓑ Ⓒ Ⓓ   35 Ⓐ Ⓑ Ⓒ Ⓓ   37 Ⓐ Ⓑ Ⓒ Ⓓ   39 Ⓐ Ⓑ Ⓒ Ⓓ

34 Ⓐ Ⓑ Ⓒ Ⓓ   36 Ⓐ Ⓑ Ⓒ Ⓓ   38 Ⓐ Ⓑ Ⓒ Ⓓ   40 Ⓐ Ⓑ Ⓒ Ⓓ

STOP

Name _____

Date _____ Class _____

8

A HELP WANTED ADS

Look at the Help Wanted ads. Choose the correct answer.

> **CASHIERS**
> FT & PT. $11/hr. Exper. pref.
> Apply in person. M-F 9am-1pm.
> Save-Mart. 2640 Central Ave.
>
> **DRIVERS**
> FT. 40 hr/wk. Excel. salary.
> Exper. req. A-1 Car Rental
> Company. Must have own trans.
> Call 714-293-4444.
>
> **OFFICE ASSISTANT**
> PT. M-F eves 6-8. Sat. 9-11am.
> Excel. typing skills req. Tip Top
> Travel. Call Sheila at 714-592-7000.
>
> **DATA ENTRY CLERK**
> FT entry-level position.
> Req. good math skills. Will train.
> Excel. benefits. Lifeco Insurance.
> Call 714-938-3350.

Example:

Which company only has a part-time job available?

- Ⓐ Save-Mart.
- Ⓑ A-1 Car Rental Company.
- Ⓒ Lifeco Insurance.
- Ⓓ Tip Top Travel.   Ⓐ Ⓑ Ⓒ ●

1. Which ad gives information about the salary?
   - Ⓐ The ad for drivers.
   - Ⓑ The ad for an office assistant.
   - Ⓒ The ad for cashiers.
   - Ⓓ The ad for a data entry clerk.

2. Victor wants to apply for a job as a driver. What does he have to do?
   - Ⓐ He has to call Save-Mart.
   - Ⓑ He has to call 714-938-3350.
   - Ⓒ He has to call 714-592-7000.
   - Ⓓ He has to call 714-293-4444.

3. How many hours per week does the office assistant work?
   - Ⓐ 10 hours per week.
   - Ⓑ 12 hours per week.
   - Ⓒ 14 hours per week.
   - Ⓓ 40 hours per week.

4. What does a person need for the job at Lifeco Insurance?
   - Ⓐ Math skills.
   - Ⓑ Excellent typing skills.
   - Ⓒ Experience as a cashier.
   - Ⓓ Transportation.

5. Which sentence ISN'T true about the jobs at Save-Mart?
   - Ⓐ Experience is preferred.
   - Ⓑ A person doesn't have to call first to apply for a job.
   - Ⓒ Experience is required.
   - Ⓓ There are part-time and full-time jobs available.

1 Ⓐ Ⓑ Ⓒ Ⓓ   3 Ⓐ Ⓑ Ⓒ Ⓓ   5 Ⓐ Ⓑ Ⓒ Ⓓ

2 Ⓐ Ⓑ Ⓒ Ⓓ   4 Ⓐ Ⓑ Ⓒ Ⓓ

Go to the next page →

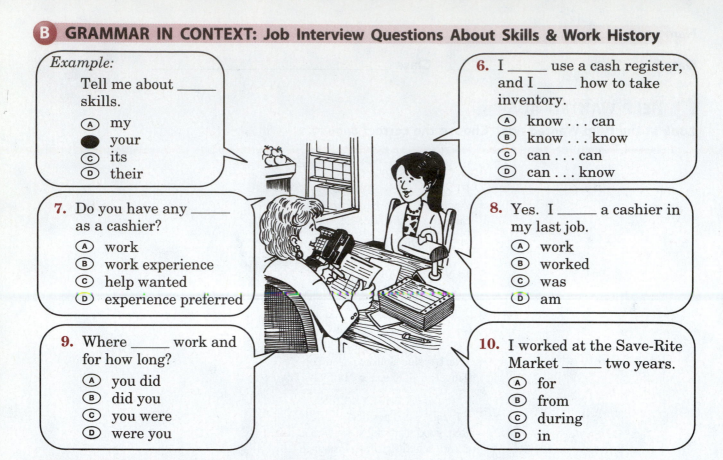

Example:
Tell me about _____ skills.
- Ⓐ my
- ● your
- Ⓒ its
- Ⓓ their

6. I _____ use a cash register, and I _____ how to take inventory.
- Ⓐ know . . . can
- Ⓑ know . . . know
- Ⓒ can . . . can
- Ⓓ can . . . know

7. Do you have any _____ as a cashier?
- Ⓐ work
- Ⓑ work experience
- Ⓒ help wanted
- Ⓓ experience preferred

8. Yes. I _____ a cashier in my last job.
- Ⓐ work
- Ⓑ worked
- Ⓒ was
- Ⓓ am

9. Where _____ work and for how long?
- Ⓐ you did
- Ⓑ did you
- Ⓒ you were
- Ⓓ were you

10. I worked at the Save-Rite Market _____ two years.
- Ⓐ for
- Ⓑ from
- Ⓒ during
- Ⓓ in

C **DESCRIBING A WORK SCHEDULE**

Look at Maria Perdomo's work schedule. Choose the correct answer.

WORK SCHEDULE		SEPTEMBER					
	SUN	MON	TUE	WED	THU	FRI	SAT
Start	12:00 PM	8:30 AM	8:30 AM		9:15 AM	9:15 AM	7:45 AM
End	9:00 PM	2:30 PM	2:30 PM		6:15 PM	6:15 PM	4:45 PM

Example:

How many days does she work this week?
- Ⓐ Four.
- Ⓑ Five.
- ● Six.
- Ⓓ Seven.

11. Which day is her day off?
- Ⓐ Monday.
- Ⓑ Wednesday.
- Ⓒ Saturday.
- Ⓓ Sunday.

12. What time does she begin work on Thursday?
- Ⓐ 9:15 AM.
- Ⓑ 6:15 PM.
- Ⓒ 8:30 AM.
- Ⓓ 12:00 PM.

13. What time does she finish work on Tuesday?
- Ⓐ 8:30 AM.
- Ⓑ 6:15 PM.
- Ⓒ 4:45 PM.
- Ⓓ 2:30 PM.

14. How many hours does she work on Friday?
- Ⓐ Six.
- Ⓑ Eight.
- Ⓒ Nine.
- Ⓓ Ten.

15. What is the total number of hours she works this week?
- Ⓐ 35.
- Ⓓ 40.
- Ⓒ 48.
- Ⓓ 50.

6 Ⓐ Ⓑ Ⓒ Ⓓ   9 Ⓐ Ⓑ Ⓒ Ⓓ   12 Ⓐ Ⓑ Ⓒ Ⓓ   15 Ⓐ Ⓑ Ⓒ Ⓓ

7 Ⓐ Ⓑ Ⓒ Ⓓ   10 Ⓐ Ⓑ Ⓒ Ⓓ   13 Ⓐ Ⓑ Ⓒ Ⓓ

8 Ⓐ Ⓑ Ⓒ Ⓓ   11 Ⓐ Ⓑ Ⓒ Ⓓ   14 Ⓐ Ⓑ Ⓒ Ⓓ

Go to the next page ⟹

D **GRAMMAR IN CONTEXT: Calling In Sick & Late; Requesting a Schedule Change**

Ex: Hello, Ms. Pratt. This is Ted Simon. I'm afraid I _____ come to work today.
- ● can't
- Ⓑ can
- Ⓒ have
- Ⓓ can to

16. What's the _____, Ted?
- Ⓐ with you
- Ⓑ sick
- Ⓒ why
- Ⓓ matter

17. _____ feel very sick.
- Ⓐ I
- Ⓑ I'm
- Ⓒ You
- Ⓓ You're

18. Okay. _____ come to work today.
- Ⓐ Don't have to
- Ⓑ You don't have to
- Ⓒ I have to
- Ⓓ I don't have to

19. Ms. Pratt? This is Debbie Simpson. _____ be late for work this morning.
- Ⓐ I'll arrive
- Ⓑ I'm going to arrive
- Ⓒ I'm going to
- Ⓓ I'm going

What happened?

20. My bus _____ a flat tire. I _____ wait for another bus.
- Ⓐ has . . . have to
- Ⓑ have . . . has to
- Ⓒ has . . . has to
- Ⓓ have . . . have to

Don't worry about it, Debbie. I'll see you when you get here.

Excuse me, Mr. Hunter. Can I possibly change my work schedule for next week?

21. What _____ change?
- Ⓐ you want
- Ⓑ do you want
- Ⓒ you want to
- Ⓓ do you want to

22. I'd like to change my _____ to Tuesday. I have to take my children to the doctor that day.
- Ⓐ off day
- Ⓑ day off
- Ⓒ sick day
- Ⓓ weekend day

23. I understand. Yes, you have my _____.
- Ⓐ application
- Ⓑ schedule
- Ⓒ permission
- Ⓓ change

Go to the next page ⟶

16 Ⓐ Ⓑ Ⓒ Ⓓ   18 Ⓐ Ⓑ Ⓒ Ⓓ   20 Ⓐ Ⓑ Ⓒ Ⓓ   22 Ⓐ Ⓑ Ⓒ Ⓓ

17 Ⓐ Ⓑ Ⓒ Ⓓ   19 Ⓐ Ⓑ Ⓒ Ⓓ   21 Ⓐ Ⓑ Ⓒ Ⓓ   23 Ⓐ Ⓑ Ⓒ Ⓓ   **35** ●

ACCIDENT REPORT

1. Name of Employee / Injured Person	2. Job Title

3. Sex	4. Date of Birth	5. SSN

6. Day, Date, & Time of Occurrence	7. Location of Accident

8. Description of Injury (Part of body injured & nature of injury)

9. What was the accident and how did it occur?

10. Safety Equipment or Procedures Being Used at Time of Accident

11. Contributing Factors (e.g., lack of training)

12. What do you recommend to prevent this accident in the future?

13. Name & Position of Witness(es)	14. Name of Physician	15. Employee's Signature

Look at the information. Choose the correct line on the form.

24. Shipping department
    - (A) Line 2
    - (B) Line 6
    - (C) Line 7
    - (D) Line 8

25. Friday, 2/10/18, 4:15 PM
    - (A) Line 3
    - (B) Line 4
    - (C) Line 5
    - (D) Line 6

26. I broke my right foot.
    - (A) Line 7
    - (B) Line 8
    - (C) Line 9
    - (D) Line 11

27. A big box fell off the forklift and dropped on my foot.
    - (A) Line 7
    - (B) Line 8
    - (C) Line 9
    - (D) Line 10

28. Michael Fuentes, stock clerk
    - (A) Line 1
    - (B) Line 2
    - (C) Line 10
    - (D) Line 13

29. The company should buy stronger protective shoes for employees in the shipping department.
    - (A) Line 12
    - (B) Line 11
    - (C) Line 10
    - (D) Line 9

24 (A) (B) (C) (D) 26 (A) (B) (C) (D) 28 (A) (B) (C) (D)
25 (A) (B) (C) (D) 27 (A) (B) (C) (D) 29 (A) (B) (C) (D)

Go to the next page ⇨

F READING: A Paycheck Stub

```
APRIL COMPANY                    RIZAL, J.                    EMP. NO. 60159
=============================================================================
PAY PERIOD ENDING         RATE          HOURS              EARNINGS
     120718               14.00           40                560.00
=============================================================================

FED TAX       47.04                    EARNINGS             560.00
FICA/MED      36.96                    TAXES                 99.12
STATE TAX     15.12                    DEDUCTIONS            60.48
HEALTH        60.48
                                       NET PAY              400.40
-----------------------------------------------------------------------------
APRIL COMPANY                               CHECK NO. 16889
                                            DATE ISSUED 121718

Pay to      JOSE RIZAL                            $400.40
FOUR HUNDRED DOLLARS AND FORTY CENTS

                                            Dee Boss
```

Look at the paycheck stub. Choose the correct answer.

30. What is Mr. Rizal's salary?
- Ⓐ 40 hours a week.
- Ⓑ $14.00 per hour.
- Ⓒ $400.40 per year.
- Ⓓ $560.00 per year.

31. How much did he earn during this pay period?
- Ⓐ $560.00.
- Ⓑ $14.00.
- Ⓒ $40.00.
- Ⓓ $99.12.

32. How much was the deduction for state taxes?
- Ⓐ $60.48.
- Ⓑ $47.04.
- Ⓒ $36.96.
- Ⓓ $15.12.

33. How much pay did Mr. Rizal take home after deductions?
- Ⓐ $560.00.
- Ⓑ $400.40.
- Ⓒ $40 per hour.
- Ⓓ $14.00.

G CLOZE READING: Nonverbal Behavior at the Job Interview

Choose the correct answers to complete the story.

The information you give at a job interview is important, but your nonverbal behavior is also important. You should dress [neat Ⓐ / neatly ● / sloppily Ⓒ] [34]. Shake hands [to Ⓐ / with Ⓑ / for Ⓒ] [34] the interviewer firmly. A firm handshake shows that you are [friend Ⓐ / friends Ⓑ / friendly Ⓒ] [35] and confident. Make "eye contact." Look at the interviewer [direct Ⓐ / directly Ⓑ / director Ⓒ] [36]. Don't speak too quickly, and don't speak too loudly or too [softly Ⓐ / softer Ⓑ / soft Ⓒ] [37]. And don't forget to smile!

....

30 Ⓐ Ⓑ Ⓒ Ⓓ	33 Ⓐ Ⓑ Ⓒ Ⓓ	36 Ⓐ Ⓑ Ⓒ Ⓓ
31 Ⓐ Ⓑ Ⓒ Ⓓ	34 Ⓐ Ⓑ Ⓒ Ⓓ	37 Ⓐ Ⓑ Ⓒ Ⓓ
32 Ⓐ Ⓑ Ⓒ Ⓓ	35 Ⓐ Ⓑ Ⓒ Ⓓ	

Go to the next page

Read and listen to the questions. Then listen to the conversation and answer the questions.

38. What kind of position is the person applying for?
  Ⓐ A job as a cashier.
  Ⓑ An office position.
  Ⓒ A position in a supermarket.
  Ⓓ A job in a computer factory.

39. Where is the conversation taking place?
  Ⓐ At the Larsen Real Estate Agency.
  Ⓑ At the Citywide Supermarket.
  Ⓒ At Landmark Data Management.
  Ⓓ At the Johnson Insurance Company.

40. How many years of work experience does the applicant have?
  Ⓐ 1 year.
  Ⓑ 2 years.
  Ⓒ 3 years.
  Ⓓ 6 years.

I WRITING: A Job Application Form

Complete this form about yourself.

APPLICATION FOR EMPLOYMENT

Name _____ Social Security Number_____

Address _____
    Street   City   State   ZIP Code

Phone No. (   ) _____ Age (if under 21) _____ Birth Date (if under 21) ___/___/___
                                                               Month Day Year

Position Desired _____ Salary Desired _____ Date you can start _____

EDUCATION

Type of School	Name	Location	Years Completed	Graduated?
High School				
College				
Other				

EMPLOYMENT (Start with present or most recent employer)

Date (Month/Year)	Name and Address of Employer	Position	Salary
From To			
From To			
From To			

Date _____ Signature _____

J SPEAKING ASSESSMENT

I can ask and answer these questions:

Ask Answer
☐ ☐ What kind of job are you looking for?
☐ ☐ Tell me about your skills and abilities.
☐ ☐ Tell me about your previous education.
☐ ☐ Tell me a little about yourself.

Ask Answer
☐ ☐ Are you currently employed?
☐ ☐ Tell me about your work history.
☐ ☐ Why do you want to work here?
☐ ☐ Do you have any questions about the position?

STOP

9

Name _____

Date _____ **Class** _____

Choose the correct answer.

1. He took _____ for his headache.
- Ⓐ a cotton ball
- Ⓑ aspirin
- Ⓒ a band-aid
- Ⓓ adhesive tape

2. I cut my finger. Could you please get _____ from the first-aid kit?
- Ⓐ a band-aid
- Ⓑ a piece of paper
- Ⓒ a cotton ball
- Ⓓ an ACE bandage

3. You should put some _____ on that cut.
- Ⓐ ice cream
- Ⓑ toothpaste
- Ⓒ aspirin
- Ⓓ antibiotic ointment

4. I'm going to clean the wound with _____.
- Ⓐ adhesive tape
- Ⓑ a napkin
- Ⓒ an antiseptic cleansing wipe
- Ⓓ a band-aid

5. The doctor used _____ to take the splinter out of my finger.
- Ⓐ a knife
- Ⓑ a screwdriver
- Ⓒ scissors
- Ⓓ tweezers

6. The school nurse wrapped my ankle with _____.
- Ⓐ an ACE bandage
- Ⓑ adhesive tape
- Ⓒ toilet paper
- Ⓓ an antiseptic cleansing wipe

7. You scraped your knee. I'm going to put on _____.
- Ⓐ adhesive tape
- Ⓑ a sterile gauze dressing pad
- Ⓒ a cotton ball
- Ⓓ an ACE bandage

8. Attach the gauze pad with _____.
- Ⓐ adhesive tape
- Ⓑ an ACE bandage
- Ⓒ a string
- Ⓓ a band-aid

1 Ⓐ Ⓑ Ⓒ Ⓓ   3 Ⓐ Ⓑ Ⓒ Ⓓ   5 Ⓐ Ⓑ Ⓒ Ⓓ   7 Ⓐ Ⓑ Ⓒ Ⓓ

2 Ⓐ Ⓑ Ⓒ Ⓓ   4 Ⓐ Ⓑ Ⓒ Ⓓ   6 Ⓐ Ⓑ Ⓒ Ⓓ   8 Ⓐ Ⓑ Ⓒ Ⓓ

Go to the next page ⟩

B GRAMMAR IN CONTEXT: Calling 911

Choose the correct answer to complete the conversations.

Emergency Operator.

9. I want to _____ a robbery!
- Ⓐ do
- Ⓑ catch
- Ⓒ report
- Ⓓ make

10. _____ the address?
- Ⓐ When is
- Ⓑ Who is
- Ⓒ How is
- Ⓓ What is

241 Central Avenue, Apartment 5.

11. And please tell me _____.
- Ⓐ who happened
- Ⓑ when it's happening
- Ⓒ what happened
- Ⓓ what's going to happen

12. Burglars broke into our apartment while we _____.
- Ⓐ working
- Ⓑ were working
- Ⓒ work
- Ⓓ works

13. Okay. We'll send a patrol car _____.
- Ⓐ right away
- Ⓑ yesterday
- Ⓒ next month
- Ⓓ every day

Thank you.

This is the Fairfax Emergency Center. You're on a recorded line.

14. We need _____ at 650 Main Street!
- Ⓐ an emergency
- Ⓑ a prescription
- Ⓒ a first-aid kit
- Ⓓ an ambulance

What's the emergency?

15. I think my father is having _____.
- Ⓐ a very bad cold
- Ⓑ an upset stomach
- Ⓒ a heart attack
- Ⓓ an earache

An emergency vehicle is on the way.

Thank you.

9 Ⓐ Ⓑ Ⓒ Ⓓ   11 Ⓐ Ⓑ Ⓒ Ⓓ   13 Ⓐ Ⓑ Ⓒ Ⓓ   15 Ⓐ Ⓑ Ⓒ Ⓓ

10 Ⓐ Ⓑ Ⓒ Ⓓ   12 Ⓐ Ⓑ Ⓒ Ⓓ   14 Ⓐ Ⓑ Ⓒ Ⓓ

Go to the next page ➡

C **GRAMMAR IN CONTEXT: Describing a Suspect's Physical Characteristics to the Police**

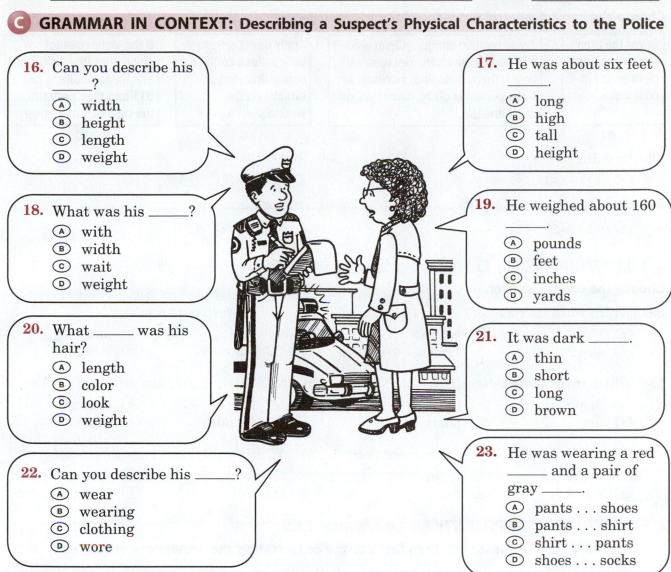

16. Can you describe his _____?
Ⓐ width
Ⓑ height
Ⓒ length
Ⓓ weight

17. He was about six feet _____.
Ⓐ long
Ⓑ high
Ⓒ tall
Ⓓ height

18. What was his _____?
Ⓐ with
Ⓑ width
Ⓒ wait
Ⓓ weight

19. He weighed about 160 _____.
Ⓐ pounds
Ⓑ feet
Ⓒ inches
Ⓓ yards

20. What _____ was his hair?
Ⓐ length
Ⓑ color
Ⓒ look
Ⓓ weight

21. It was dark _____.
Ⓐ thin
Ⓑ short
Ⓒ long
Ⓓ brown

22. Can you describe his _____?
Ⓐ wear
Ⓑ wearing
Ⓒ clothing
Ⓓ wore

23. He was wearing a red _____ and a pair of gray _____.
Ⓐ pants . . . shoes
Ⓑ pants . . . shirt
Ⓒ shirt . . . pants
Ⓓ shoes . . . socks

D **READING: Warning Labels on Household Products**

Choose the correct warning label for each instruction.

Do not use with other household chemicals.	Avoid direct contact. Wear rubber gloves.	Harmful if swallowed.	Avoid prolonged breathing of vapors.
A	B	C	D

24. Do not eat or drink.
Ⓐ Ⓑ Ⓒ Ⓓ

26. Use only in well-ventilated areas. Avoid fumes.
Ⓐ Ⓑ Ⓒ Ⓓ

25. Do not get on skin.
Ⓐ Ⓑ Ⓒ Ⓓ

27. Do not mix together with other products.
Ⓐ Ⓑ Ⓒ Ⓓ

. . . .

16 Ⓐ Ⓑ Ⓒ Ⓓ   19 Ⓐ Ⓑ Ⓒ Ⓓ   22 Ⓐ Ⓑ Ⓒ Ⓓ   25 Ⓐ Ⓑ Ⓒ Ⓓ

17 Ⓐ Ⓑ Ⓒ Ⓓ   20 Ⓐ Ⓑ Ⓒ Ⓓ   23 Ⓐ Ⓑ Ⓒ Ⓓ   26 Ⓐ Ⓑ Ⓒ Ⓓ

18 Ⓐ Ⓑ Ⓒ Ⓓ   21 Ⓐ Ⓑ Ⓒ Ⓓ   24 Ⓐ Ⓑ Ⓒ Ⓓ   27 Ⓐ Ⓑ Ⓒ Ⓓ

Go to the next page ⟩

E READING: First Aid Procedures

Choose the correct medical procedure for each emergency.

Cover the area with a cool wet cloth or put in cool water.	Try to remove stinger. Clean wound and apply cold cloth. Get medical help if there is itching, swelling, or if the person is dizzy, nauseous, or can't breathe.	Apply direct pressure with a clean cloth or sterile dressing directly on the wound.	If the victim cannot speak, breathe, or cough, ask for someone to call 911 and then perform the Heimlich maneuver.
A	**B**	**C**	**D**

28. bleeding
    Ⓐ Ⓑ Ⓒ Ⓓ

29. choking
    Ⓐ Ⓑ Ⓒ Ⓓ

30. bee sting
    Ⓐ Ⓑ Ⓒ Ⓓ

31. minor burn
    Ⓐ Ⓑ Ⓒ Ⓓ

F LEARNING SKILL: Categorizing Words; Word Sets

Choose the correct answer.

32. Which word isn't a *color*?
    Ⓐ blue   Ⓒ white
    Ⓑ shirt   Ⓓ brown

33. Which word doesn't describe *weight*?
    Ⓐ heavy   Ⓒ light
    Ⓑ fat   Ⓓ short

34. Which word isn't a *form of transportation*?
    Ⓐ telephone Ⓒ train
    Ⓑ airplane   Ⓓ bus

35. Which word isn't a *season*?
    Ⓐ spring   Ⓒ snowing
    Ⓑ summer   Ⓓ winter

36. Which word isn't a *month*?
    Ⓐ May   Ⓒ August
    Ⓑ Monday   Ⓓ June

37. Which word doesn't describe *height*?
    Ⓐ heavy   Ⓒ short
    Ⓑ tall   Ⓓ medium height

G LISTENING ASSESSMENT: An Emergency Call

Read and listen to the questions. Then listen to the conversation and answer the questions.

38. When did the person fall?
    Ⓐ While she was on a trip.
    Ⓑ While she was in her apartment.
    Ⓒ While she was on the phone.
    Ⓓ While she was walking down the stairs.

39. What's their address?
    Ⓐ 13 East Street.
    Ⓑ 13 West Street.
    Ⓒ 30 East Street.
    Ⓓ 30 West Street.

40. Where is their apartment?
    Ⓐ On the 5th floor.
    Ⓑ On the 6th floor.
    Ⓒ Apartment 6-C.
    Ⓓ Apartment 6-G.

H WRITING ASSESSMENT: Fill Out the Form

Name _____

Height _____ Weight _____

Hair Color _____ Eye Color _____

I SPEAKING ASSESSMENT

I can ask and answer these questions:

Ask Answer
☐ ☐ What's your height?
☐ ☐ What's your hair color?
☐ ☐ What color are your eyes?
☐ ☐ What are you wearing today?

- -

28 Ⓐ Ⓑ Ⓒ Ⓓ   31 Ⓐ Ⓑ Ⓒ Ⓓ   35 Ⓐ Ⓑ Ⓒ Ⓓ   38 Ⓐ Ⓑ Ⓒ Ⓓ

29 Ⓐ Ⓑ Ⓒ Ⓓ   32 Ⓐ Ⓑ Ⓒ Ⓓ   36 Ⓐ Ⓑ Ⓒ Ⓓ   39 Ⓐ Ⓑ Ⓒ Ⓓ

30 Ⓐ Ⓑ Ⓒ Ⓓ   33 Ⓐ Ⓑ Ⓒ Ⓓ   37 Ⓐ Ⓑ Ⓒ Ⓓ   40 Ⓐ Ⓑ Ⓒ Ⓓ

34 Ⓐ Ⓑ Ⓒ Ⓓ

STOP

Name _____

Date _____ Class _____

10

A   HOUSING ADS

Look at the classified ads for housing. Choose the correct answer.

2 BR 1 BA, d/w, $950 incl util. 273-4651.	3BR 2 BA, big apt, d/w, cac, w/d, $1400 + util. Avail 9/15. 727-4981.
1 BR 1 BA, w/w, catv, nr hospital, $750 + util. Avail 10/1. 589-7315.	2 BR 1 1/2 BA, pkg, nr airport, d/w, incl catv, $875 + elec. 863-4193.

1. You're looking for a one-bedroom apartment. Which number will you call?
    - Ⓐ 273-4651.
    - Ⓑ 589-7315.
    - Ⓒ 727-4981.
    - Ⓓ 863-4193.

2. You need an apartment with two bathrooms. Which number will you call?
    - Ⓐ 863-4193.
    - Ⓑ 273-4651.
    - Ⓒ 589-7315.
    - Ⓓ 727-4981.

3. Which apartment includes utilities?
    - Ⓐ The 2-bedroom apartment with 1 bath.
    - Ⓑ The 2-bedroom apartment with 1 1/2 baths.
    - Ⓒ The 3-bedroom apartment.
    - Ⓓ The 1-bedroom apartment.

4. Which apartment doesn't have a dishwasher?
    - Ⓐ The 2-bedroom apartment with 1 bath.
    - Ⓑ The 2-bedroom apartment with 1 1/2 baths.
    - Ⓒ The 1-bedroom apartment.
    - Ⓓ The 3-bedroom apartment.

5. Which apartment is available on Sept. 15?
    - Ⓐ The 2-bedroom apartment with 1 bath.
    - Ⓑ The 2-bedroom apartment with 1 1/2 baths.
    - Ⓒ The 1-bedroom apartment.
    - Ⓓ The 3-bedroom apartment.

6. How many of these apartments have cable TV?
    - Ⓐ One.
    - Ⓑ Two.
    - Ⓒ Three.
    - Ⓓ Four.

7. How much is the rent for the apartment near the hospital?
    - Ⓐ $750 plus utilities.
    - Ⓑ $875 plus electricity.
    - Ⓒ $950 plus utilities.
    - Ⓓ $1400 plus utilities.

8. What does the 3-bedroom apartment have that the other apartments don't have?
    - Ⓐ Two bathrooms and a dishwasher.
    - Ⓑ A dishwasher and central air conditioning.
    - Ⓒ A dishwasher and a washer and dryer.
    - Ⓓ A washer and dryer and central air conditioning.

9. You're a pilot. You and a friend are looking for an apartment. Which number will you call?
    - Ⓐ 863-4193.
    - Ⓑ 727-4981.
    - Ⓒ 273-4651.
    - Ⓓ 589-7315.

10. What does the 1-bedroom apartment have that the other apartments don't have?
    - Ⓐ Cable TV.
    - Ⓑ Wall-to-wall carpeting.
    - Ⓒ A dishwasher.
    - Ⓓ A washer and dryer.

1 Ⓐ Ⓑ Ⓒ Ⓓ   4 Ⓐ Ⓑ Ⓒ Ⓓ   7 Ⓐ Ⓑ Ⓒ Ⓓ   10 Ⓐ Ⓑ Ⓒ Ⓓ

2 Ⓐ Ⓑ Ⓒ Ⓓ   5 Ⓐ Ⓑ Ⓒ Ⓓ   8 Ⓐ Ⓑ Ⓒ Ⓓ

3 Ⓐ Ⓑ Ⓒ Ⓓ   6 Ⓐ Ⓑ Ⓒ Ⓓ   9 Ⓐ Ⓑ Ⓒ Ⓓ

Go to the next page ▷

Choose the correct answer to complete the conversation.

11. Is the apartment furnished
_____ unfurnished?
Ⓐ and
Ⓑ but
Ⓒ or
Ⓓ with

12. It's unfurnished. _____
any furniture in the unit.
Ⓐ Isn't
Ⓑ There isn't
Ⓒ Aren't
Ⓓ There aren't

13. Is there public _____
nearby?
Ⓐ communication
Ⓑ location
Ⓒ station
Ⓓ transportation

14. Yes. There's a bus stop
_____ the corner.
Ⓐ around
Ⓑ between
Ⓒ next
Ⓓ across

15. _____ is the rent?
Ⓐ How many
Ⓑ What does it cost
Ⓒ How much
Ⓓ What is the price

16. _____
Ⓐ On the third floor.
Ⓑ On the first day of the
month.
Ⓒ Every month.
Ⓓ $800 a month.

17. _____ a security deposit?
Ⓐ Are you
Ⓑ Is there
Ⓒ Am I
Ⓓ Is it

18. Yes. We require one
month rent in advance
when you _____ the lease.
Ⓐ sign
Ⓑ print
Ⓒ leave
Ⓓ signature

19. Is the building in _____
neighborhood?
Ⓐ a dangerous
Ⓑ an empty
Ⓒ an inconvenient
Ⓓ a convenient

20. Yes. _____ many stores in
the neighborhood, and
_____ a school nearby.
Ⓐ There is . . . there's
Ⓑ There is . . . there are
Ⓒ There are . . . there's
Ⓓ There are . . . there are

21. Are pets _____?
Ⓐ loud
Ⓑ allowed
Ⓒ may they
Ⓓ can we

22. Yes. Dogs and cats _____.
Ⓐ have permission
Ⓑ is permitted
Ⓒ are permitted
Ⓓ are you allowed

11 Ⓐ Ⓑ Ⓒ Ⓓ   14 Ⓐ Ⓑ Ⓒ Ⓓ   17 Ⓐ Ⓑ Ⓒ Ⓓ   20 Ⓐ Ⓑ Ⓒ Ⓓ
12 Ⓐ Ⓑ Ⓒ Ⓓ   15 Ⓐ Ⓑ Ⓒ Ⓓ   18 Ⓐ Ⓑ Ⓒ Ⓓ   21 Ⓐ Ⓑ Ⓒ Ⓓ
13 Ⓐ Ⓑ Ⓒ Ⓓ   16 Ⓐ Ⓑ Ⓒ Ⓓ   19 Ⓐ Ⓑ Ⓒ Ⓓ   22 Ⓐ Ⓑ Ⓒ Ⓓ

Go to the next page ⟶

Name _____ Date _____

23. Hello. This is David Lee, the new tenant in Apartment 412. There are _____ in my apartment.
- (A) broken
- (B) a problem
- (C) many repairs
- (D) many problems

24. What's the _____?
- (A) matter
- (B) repair
- (C) problems
- (D) troubles

25. The doorbell is broken. _____
- (A) It doesn't open.
- (B) It doesn't lock.
- (C) It doesn't ring.
- (D) It doesn't close.

26. _____ And what else?
- (A) You see.
- (B) I see.
- (C) It sees.
- (D) We see.

I understand.

27. The oven doesn't light. _____
- (A) The kitchen is dark.
- (B) I can't bake.
- (C) I can't see inside the oven.
- (D) My food always burns.

28. The bathtub is cracked. _____
- (A) There's water on the bathroom floor.
- (B) The roof is leaking.
- (C) The sink is leaking.
- (D) There's water on the kitchen floor.

29. Okay. _____
- (A) Else?
- (B) Other?
- (C) Anything?
- (D) Anything else?

30. Yes. One more thing. The kitchen sink is clogged. _____
- (A) The water is too hot.
- (B) The water is too cold.
- (C) The water doesn't go down the drain.
- (D) Water doesn't come out of the faucet.

Thank you very much.

31. All right. I'll send someone to _____ everything right away.
- (A) repair
- (B) break
- (C) fixes
- (D) will fix

32. You're welcome, and I _____ for the inconvenience.
- (A) please
- (B) thank you
- (C) sorry
- (D) apologize

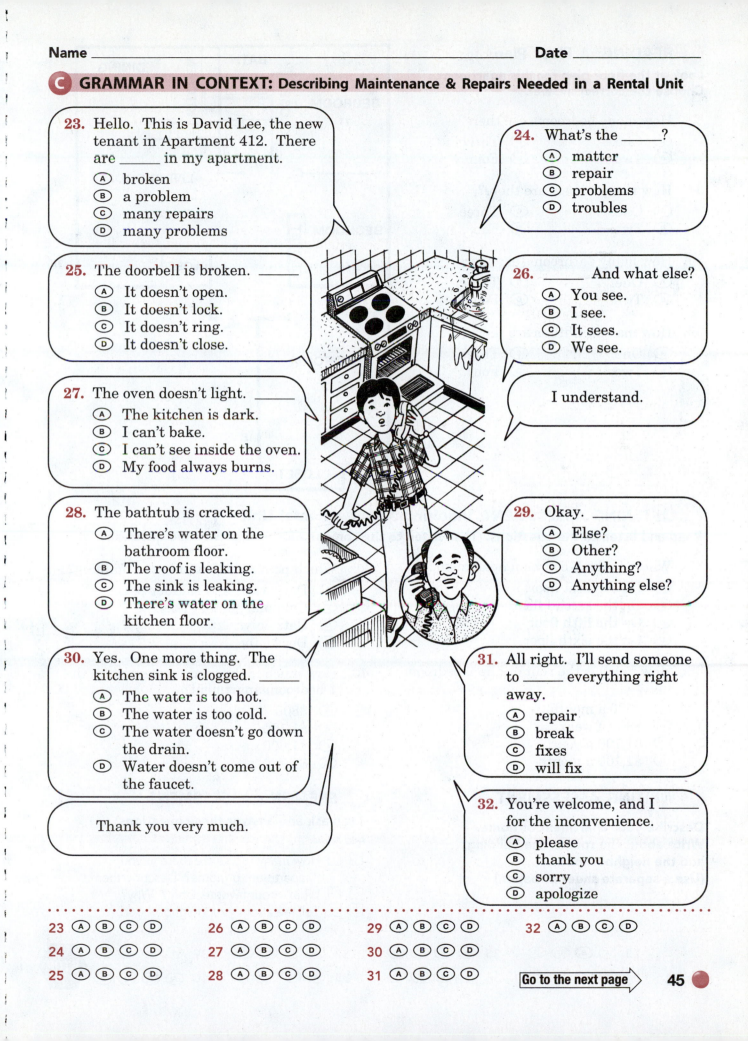

23 Ⓐ Ⓑ Ⓒ Ⓓ   26 Ⓐ Ⓑ Ⓒ Ⓓ   29 Ⓐ Ⓑ Ⓒ Ⓓ   32 Ⓐ Ⓑ Ⓒ Ⓓ
24 Ⓐ Ⓑ Ⓒ Ⓓ   27 Ⓐ Ⓑ Ⓒ Ⓓ   30 Ⓐ Ⓑ Ⓒ Ⓓ
25 Ⓐ Ⓑ Ⓒ Ⓓ   28 Ⓐ Ⓑ Ⓒ Ⓓ   31 Ⓐ Ⓑ Ⓒ Ⓓ

D READING: A Floor Plan

Look at the floor plan for this apartment.
Choose the correct answer.

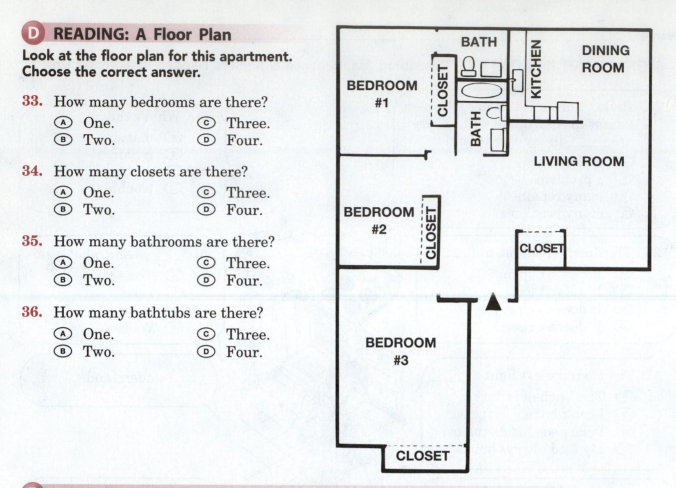

33. How many bedrooms are there?
Ⓐ One.   Ⓒ Three.
Ⓑ Two.   Ⓓ Four.

34. How many closets are there?
Ⓐ One.   Ⓒ Three.
Ⓑ Two.   Ⓓ Four.

35. How many bathrooms are there?
Ⓐ One.   Ⓒ Three.
Ⓑ Two.   Ⓓ Four.

36. How many bathtubs are there?
Ⓐ One.   Ⓒ Three.
Ⓑ Two.   Ⓓ Four.

E LISTENING ASSESSMENT: Inquiring About a Rental Unit

Read and listen to the questions. Then listen to the conversation and answer the questions.

37. Where is the 1-bedroom apartment?
Ⓐ On the first floor.
Ⓑ On the second floor.
Ⓒ On the fifth floor.
Ⓓ On the sixth floor.

38. How much is the rent on the 2-bedroom unit?
Ⓐ $800 a month.
Ⓑ $800 a week.
Ⓒ $1,100 a year.
Ⓓ $1,100 a month.

39. Which pets are allowed in the building?
Ⓐ Dogs, cats, and smaller pets.
Ⓑ Cats and smaller pets.
Ⓒ Cats only.
Ⓓ Dogs only.

40. How much is the security deposit on the 1-bedroom apartment?
Ⓐ $800
Ⓑ $1,100
Ⓒ $1,600
Ⓓ $2,200

F WRITING ASSESSMENT

Describe your apartment or home.
Write about the rooms, the building,
and the neighborhood.
(Use a separate sheet of paper.)

G SPEAKING ASSESSMENT

I can ask and answer these questions:

Ask Answer
☐ ☐ How many rooms are there in your apartment or home? Describe them.
☐ ☐ What's your favorite room? Why?
☐ ☐ Tell me about your neighborhood.

33 Ⓐ Ⓑ Ⓒ Ⓓ   35 Ⓐ Ⓑ Ⓒ Ⓓ   37 Ⓐ Ⓑ Ⓒ Ⓓ   39 Ⓐ Ⓑ Ⓒ Ⓓ
34 Ⓐ Ⓑ Ⓒ Ⓓ   36 Ⓐ Ⓑ Ⓒ Ⓓ   38 Ⓐ Ⓑ Ⓒ Ⓓ   40 Ⓐ Ⓑ Ⓒ Ⓓ

STOP

A IDENTIFYING PARTS OF THE FACE & BODY

Choose the correct answer.

Example:

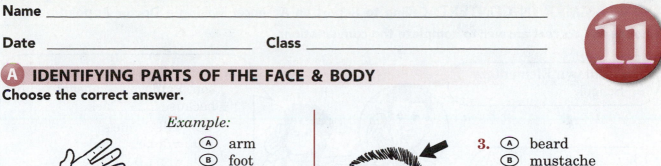

    Ⓐ arm
    Ⓑ foot
    ● hand
    Ⓓ toe

1. Ⓐ ears
    Ⓑ fingers
    Ⓒ toes
    Ⓓ lips

2. Ⓐ wrist
    Ⓑ ankle
    Ⓒ elbow
    Ⓓ arm

3. Ⓐ beard
    Ⓑ mustache
    Ⓒ eyebrow
    Ⓓ eyelash

4. Ⓐ wrist
    Ⓑ shoulder
    Ⓒ ankle
    Ⓓ elbow

5. Ⓐ hip
    Ⓑ leg
    Ⓒ shoulder
    Ⓓ thigh

B COMMON SYMPTOMS

Choose the correct answer.

6. My temperature is 102° F. I have _____.
    Ⓐ a sweater
    Ⓑ an oven
    Ⓒ high blood pressure
    Ⓓ a fever

7. Timmy needs a tissue. He has _____.
    Ⓐ a runny nose
    Ⓑ a sore throat
    Ⓒ a backache
    Ⓓ a fever

8. Carla ate too much candy. Now she has _____.
    Ⓐ an earache
    Ⓑ a toothache
    Ⓒ a cold
    Ⓓ a runny nose

9. That music was loud! I have _____.
    Ⓐ a stiff back
    Ⓑ a cold
    Ⓒ a head
    Ⓓ an earache

10. I sang all day. Now I have _____.
    Ⓐ a backache
    Ⓑ an earache
    Ⓒ a sore throat
    Ⓓ a sprained ankle

11. I think I have a cold. I have a bad _____.
    Ⓐ sneeze
    Ⓑ cough
    Ⓒ throat
    Ⓓ nose

1 Ⓐ Ⓑ Ⓒ Ⓓ   4 Ⓐ Ⓑ Ⓒ Ⓓ   7 Ⓐ Ⓑ Ⓒ Ⓓ   10 Ⓐ Ⓑ Ⓒ Ⓓ

2 Ⓐ Ⓑ Ⓒ Ⓓ   5 Ⓐ Ⓑ Ⓒ Ⓓ   8 Ⓐ Ⓑ Ⓒ Ⓓ   11 Ⓐ Ⓑ Ⓒ Ⓓ

3 Ⓐ Ⓑ Ⓒ Ⓓ   6 Ⓐ Ⓑ Ⓒ Ⓓ   9 Ⓐ Ⓑ Ⓒ Ⓓ

Go to the next page ⟩

GRAMMAR IN CONTEXT: Calling to Report an Absence; Making a Doctor Appointment

Choose the correct answer to complete the conversations.

Woodlawn Elementary School.

12. Hello. This is Amy Long. My son, Paul, _____ absent today because _____ sick.
Ⓐ will . . . he's
Ⓑ will be . . . he's
Ⓒ won't be . . . he
Ⓓ can't . . . he

13. _____ class is he in?
Ⓐ Which
Ⓑ Who
Ⓒ Where
Ⓓ When

He's in Mr. Wilson's 4th grade class.

Doctor's office.

14. Hello. This is Alicia Flores. I don't _____ well.
Ⓐ sick   Ⓒ feel
Ⓑ healthy   Ⓓ feeling

15. _____ the matter?
Ⓐ How's
Ⓑ Why's
Ⓒ Where's
Ⓓ What's

I have a very bad stomachache.

16. Do you want to make _____?
Ⓐ medicine
Ⓑ see the doctor
Ⓒ a reservation
Ⓓ an appointment

Yes, please.

17. _____ tomorrow at 2 PM?
Ⓐ Can you come in
Ⓑ Can you go
Ⓒ Are you sick
Ⓓ Is the doctor here

2 PM? Yes. Thank you.

D **PROCEDURES DURING A MEDICAL EXAM**

18. The nurse took my blood _____.
Ⓐ pulse   Ⓒ pressure
Ⓑ weight   Ⓓ temperature

20. He measured my _____ on the scale.
Ⓐ wait   Ⓒ weight
Ⓑ waist   Ⓓ pulse

19. The doctor listened to my heart with _____.
Ⓐ a scale   Ⓒ an X-ray
Ⓑ a stethoscope Ⓓ a headphone

21. She _____ my eyes, ears, nose, and throat.
Ⓐ took   Ⓒ measured
Ⓑ listened to Ⓓ examined

12 Ⓐ Ⓑ Ⓒ Ⓓ   15 Ⓐ Ⓑ Ⓒ Ⓓ   18 Ⓐ Ⓑ Ⓒ Ⓓ   21 Ⓐ Ⓑ Ⓒ Ⓓ

13 Ⓐ Ⓑ Ⓒ Ⓓ   16 Ⓐ Ⓑ Ⓒ Ⓓ   19 Ⓐ Ⓑ Ⓒ Ⓓ

14 Ⓐ Ⓑ Ⓒ Ⓓ   17 Ⓐ Ⓑ Ⓒ Ⓓ   20 Ⓐ Ⓑ Ⓒ Ⓓ   Go to the next page ⟩

E COMMON PRESCRIPTION & NON-PRESCRIPTION MEDICATIONS

22. The doctor recommended _____ for the rash on my arm.
- Ⓐ anti-itch cream
- Ⓑ throat lozenges
- Ⓒ cough syrup
- Ⓓ antacid tablets

23. I'm taking _____ for my upset stomach.
- Ⓐ cough syrup
- Ⓑ antacid tablets
- Ⓒ throat lozenges
- Ⓓ aspirin

24. The doctor gave me a prescription for _____ for my throat infection.
- Ⓐ vitamins
- Ⓑ cold medicine
- Ⓒ ear drops
- Ⓓ penicillin

25. I sneeze and cough every spring, so the clinic gives me a prescription for _____.
- Ⓐ throat lozenges
- Ⓑ cough syrup
- Ⓒ allergy medication
- Ⓓ cold medicine

F READING: Medicine Label Dosages

Choose the correct medicine label for each instruction.

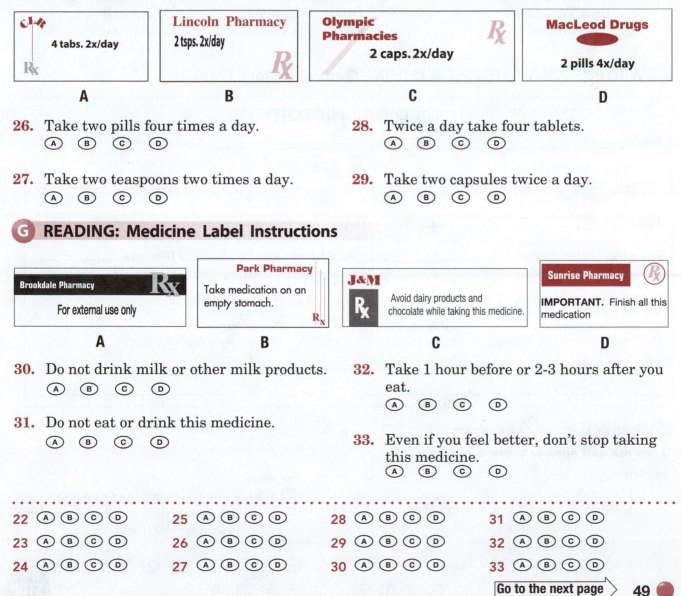

CLR 4 tabs. 2x/day **Rx**	**Lincoln Pharmacy** 2 tsps. 2x/day **Rx**	**Olympic Pharmacies** 2 caps. 2x/day **Rx**	**MacLeod Drugs** 2 pills 4x/day
A	B	C	D

26. Take two pills four times a day.
Ⓐ Ⓑ Ⓒ Ⓓ

27. Take two teaspoons two times a day.
Ⓐ Ⓑ Ⓒ Ⓓ

28. Twice a day take four tablets.
Ⓐ Ⓑ Ⓒ Ⓓ

29. Take two capsules twice a day.
Ⓐ Ⓑ Ⓒ Ⓓ

G READING: Medicine Label Instructions

Brookdale Pharmacy **Rx** For external use only	**Park Pharmacy** Take medication on an empty stomach. **Rx**	**J&M Rx** Avoid dairy products and chocolate while taking this medicine.	**Sunrise Pharmacy Rx** IMPORTANT. Finish all this medication
A	B	C	D

30. Do not drink milk or other milk products.
Ⓐ Ⓑ Ⓒ Ⓓ

31. Do not eat or drink this medicine.
Ⓐ Ⓑ Ⓒ Ⓓ

32. Take 1 hour before or 2-3 hours after you eat.
Ⓐ Ⓑ Ⓒ Ⓓ

33. Even if you feel better, don't stop taking this medicine.
Ⓐ Ⓑ Ⓒ Ⓓ

....

22 Ⓐ Ⓑ Ⓒ Ⓓ	25 Ⓐ Ⓑ Ⓒ Ⓓ	28 Ⓐ Ⓑ Ⓒ Ⓓ	31 Ⓐ Ⓑ Ⓒ Ⓓ
23 Ⓐ Ⓑ Ⓒ Ⓓ	26 Ⓐ Ⓑ Ⓒ Ⓓ	29 Ⓐ Ⓑ Ⓒ Ⓓ	32 Ⓐ Ⓑ Ⓒ Ⓓ
24 Ⓐ Ⓑ Ⓒ Ⓓ	27 Ⓐ Ⓑ Ⓒ Ⓓ	30 Ⓐ Ⓑ Ⓒ Ⓓ	33 Ⓐ Ⓑ Ⓒ Ⓓ

H CLOZE READING: A Note to the Teacher

Deer Dare Dear Mr. Harper,
Ⓐ   Ⓑ   ●

My daughter, Jenny, was present absent not ³⁴ from school yesterday
                        Ⓐ   Ⓑ   Ⓒ

reason because for ³⁵ she had a very full good bad ³⁶ stomachache and I took
Ⓐ   Ⓑ   Ⓒ   Ⓐ   Ⓑ   Ⓒ

her him it ³⁷ to the doctor.
Ⓐ   Ⓑ   Ⓒ

Sincerely,

Barbara Taylor

I LISTENING ASSESSMENT: Making a Doctor Appointment

Read and listen to the questions. Then listen to the conversation and answer the questions.

38. When did she hurt her back?
- Ⓐ Today.
- Ⓑ Yesterday.
- Ⓒ Last Tuesday.
- Ⓓ Last Thursday.

39. Where did she hurt it?
- Ⓐ At home.
- Ⓑ At the clinic.
- Ⓒ On the telephone.
- Ⓓ On the job.

40. What time does she have to be at the clinic?
- Ⓐ 7:15 AM.
- Ⓑ 7:30 AM.
- Ⓒ 7:45 AM.
- Ⓓ 7:30 PM.

J WRITING ASSESSMENT: Fill Out the Medical History Form

MEDICAL HISTORY

Name _____   Date of Birth ____ / ____ / ____
      First   M. I.   Last   Month   Day   Year

Address _____   _____ _____ _____
      Number Street   City   State   Zip Code

Telephone: Home _____   Work _____   Height _____   Weight _____

Emergency Contact: Name _____   Relationship _____   Telephone _____

Do you have:	YES	NO		YES	NO		YES	NO
heart disease?	☐	☐	allergies?	☐	☐	other problems?	☐	☐
kidney disease?	☐	☐	headaches?	☐	☐	Do you smoke?	☐	☐
high blood pressure?	☐	☐	trouble sleeping?	☐	☐	Do you drink?	☐	☐
diabetes?	☐	☐	trouble eating?	☐	☐	Are you taking medicine now?	☐	☐

If you answered Yes above, explain: _____

_____

K SPEAKING ASSESSMENT

I can ask and answer these questions:

Ask Answer
☐ ☐ How do you feel?
☐ ☐ When was your last appointment at a clinic or doctor's office?

Ask Answer
☐ ☐ Are you taking any medicine now?
☐ ☐ Is there any history of medical problems in your family? Explain.

A FAHRENHEIT & CELSIUS TEMPERATURES

Look at the thermometer. Choose the correct temperature.

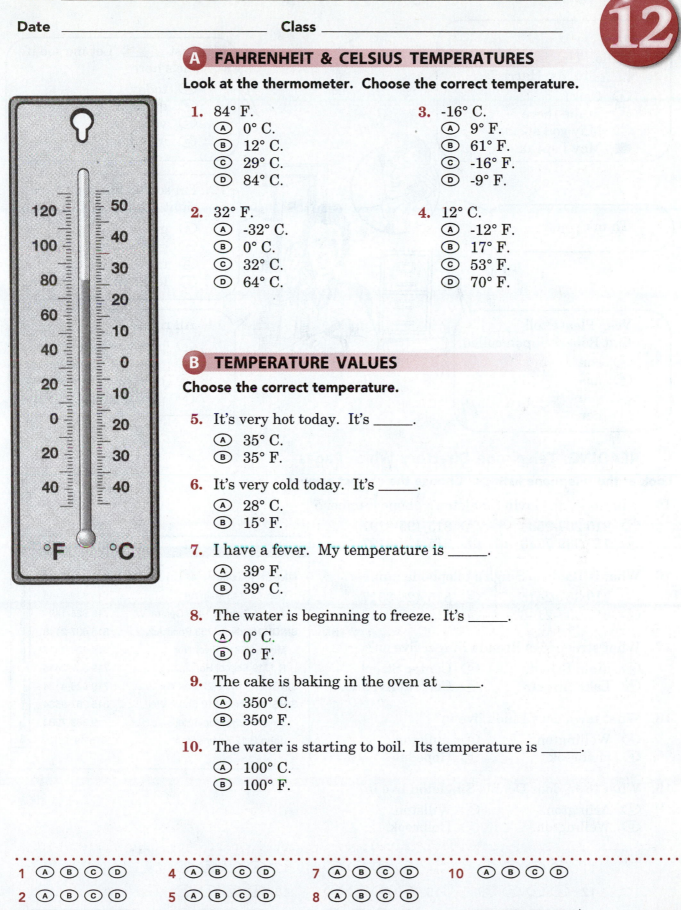

1. 84° F.
- Ⓐ 0° C.
- Ⓑ 12° C.
- Ⓒ 29° C.
- Ⓓ 84° C.

2. 32° F.
- Ⓐ -32° C.
- Ⓑ 0° C.
- Ⓒ 32° C.
- Ⓓ 64° C.

3. -16° C.
- Ⓐ 9° F.
- Ⓑ 61° F.
- Ⓒ -16° F.
- Ⓓ -9° F.

4. 12° C.
- Ⓐ -12° F.
- Ⓑ 17° F.
- Ⓒ 53° F.
- Ⓓ 70° F.

B TEMPERATURE VALUES

Choose the correct temperature.

5. It's very hot today. It's _____.
- Ⓐ 35° C.
- Ⓑ 35° F.

6. It's very cold today. It's _____.
- Ⓐ 28° C.
- Ⓑ 15° F.

7. I have a fever. My temperature is _____.
- Ⓐ 39° F.
- Ⓑ 39° C.

8. The water is beginning to freeze. It's _____.
- Ⓐ 0° C.
- Ⓑ 0° F.

9. The cake is baking in the oven at _____.
- Ⓐ 350° C.
- Ⓑ 350° F.

10. The water is starting to boil. Its temperature is _____.
- Ⓐ 100° C.
- Ⓑ 100° F.

1 Ⓐ Ⓑ Ⓒ Ⓓ   4 Ⓐ Ⓑ Ⓒ Ⓓ   7 Ⓐ Ⓑ Ⓒ Ⓓ   10 Ⓐ Ⓑ Ⓒ Ⓓ

2 Ⓐ Ⓑ Ⓒ Ⓓ   5 Ⓐ Ⓑ Ⓒ Ⓓ   8 Ⓐ Ⓑ Ⓒ Ⓓ

3 Ⓐ Ⓑ Ⓒ Ⓓ   6 Ⓐ Ⓑ Ⓒ Ⓓ   9 Ⓐ Ⓑ Ⓒ Ⓓ   Go to the next page ⟩

C GRAMMAR IN CONTEXT: Beginning & Ending a Telephone Conversation

Example:

Hello. This is Robert Simon. _____ to Ms. Harris?
- Ⓐ Can I
- Ⓑ Is she there
- Ⓒ May you speak
- ● May I speak

Thank you.

13. Yes. Please tell _____ that Robert Simon called.
- Ⓐ she
- Ⓑ me
- Ⓒ you
- Ⓓ her

11. Just _____. Let me see if she's here.
- Ⓐ today
- Ⓑ an hour
- Ⓒ you wait
- Ⓓ a moment

12. I'm sorry. She isn't here right now. Can I _____?
- Ⓐ give a message
- Ⓑ give you a message
- Ⓒ take a message
- Ⓓ leave you a message

14. All right. I'll _____.
- Ⓐ give the message
- Ⓑ give her the message
- Ⓒ give you the message
- Ⓓ give me the message

D READING: Telephone Directory White Pages

Look at the telephone listings. Choose the correct answer.

15. What is John Gavin Singleton's phone number?
- Ⓐ 815 267-9534
- Ⓒ 815 495-8197
- Ⓑ 719 389-7283
- Ⓓ 815 459-8197

16. What is Rajdeep Singh's telephone number?
- Ⓐ 719 387-2415
- Ⓒ 815 426-3317
- Ⓑ 815 637-2148
- Ⓓ 815 387-2415

17. What street does Brenda Singer live on?
- Ⓐ Main Street.
- Ⓒ Center Street.
- Ⓑ Lake Street.
- Ⓓ Central Avenue.

18. What town does Linda live in?
- Ⓐ Wellington.
- Ⓒ Willston.
- Ⓑ Holbrook.
- Ⓓ Hopedale.

19. What town does Dennis Singleton live in?
- Ⓐ Arlington.
- Ⓒ Willston.
- Ⓑ Wellington.
- Ⓓ Holbrook.

SINCLAIR—SINGLETON	649
SINGER Alexander 42 Lake Nor 815 427-7251	
Dennis 143 Main Arl 815 639-9148	
Tom & Brenda 1423 Central Wil 719 825-1491	
SINGH Hardeep 753 Pond Arl 815 637-2148	
Madan 2213 River Nor 815 426-3317	
R 1719 School Hol 719 387-2415	
SINGLER Linda 27 Oak Wil 719 828-4124	
SINGLETON D 819 Shore Wel 815 267-9534	
John E 238 Maple Hol 719 389-7283	
John G 12 Adams Hop 815 495-8197	

RESIDENCE LISTING

52

11 Ⓐ Ⓑ Ⓒ Ⓓ   14 Ⓐ Ⓑ Ⓒ Ⓓ   17 Ⓐ Ⓑ Ⓒ Ⓓ
12 Ⓐ Ⓑ Ⓒ Ⓓ   15 Ⓐ Ⓑ Ⓒ Ⓓ   18 Ⓐ Ⓑ Ⓒ Ⓓ
13 Ⓐ Ⓑ Ⓒ Ⓓ   16 Ⓐ Ⓑ Ⓒ Ⓓ   19 Ⓐ Ⓑ Ⓒ Ⓓ

Go to the next page ▷

Name _____   Date _____

E READING: Telephone Directory Government Pages & Yellow Pages

NORTHBORO TOWN OF

AMBULANCE
   Emergency Only 911
ANIMAL CONTROL 815 821-6014
BOARD OF HEALTH 815 821-6020
ELECTRIC LIGHT DEPT 815 821-6035
HIGHWAY DEPT 815 821-6040
LIBRARY 400 Main Nor 815 821-6030
PARKS & RECREATION 815 821-6018
POLICE—
   Emergency Only 911
   All Other Purposes 815 821-5000
SCHOOLS—
   Elementary—
     Eastwick 360 Main Nor 815 821-6130
   Middle School—
     Jefferson 120 Central Nor 815 821-6140
   High School–
     Lincoln 72 School Nor 815 821-6180

20. The street lamp on Hernan's street is broken. What number should he call?
- (A) 911
- (B) 815 821-5000
- (C) 815 821-6014
- (D) 815 821-6035

21. A very mean dog is running up and down the street in front of Claudia's apartment building. What number should she call?
- (A) 815 821-6020
- (B) 815 821-6018
- (C) 815 821-6040
- (D) 815 821-6014

22. The Chungs just moved to Northboro. They want to enroll their son in 10th grade. What number should they call?
- (A) 815 821-6180
- (B) 815 621-6140
- (C) 815 821-6130
- (D) 815 821-6060

23. The Hills ate at a restaurant yesterday. This morning they all have terrible stomachaches. They think the chicken at the restaurant was bad. What number should they call?
- (A) 815 821-6014
- (B) 815 821-6030
- (C) 815 821-6020
- (D) 815 821-5000

24. There's broken glass in the playground across the street from the police station. What number should you call?
- (A) 815 821-6130
- (B) 815 821-6018
- (C) 815 821-5000
- (D) 911

Pizza

Classic Pizza & Pasta
   124 Main Ple 315 469-7750
Jimmy's House of Pizza
   32 Western Ree 315 727-9123

Plants—Retail

Flowers For You
   1200 Central Ree 315 727-4124

Plumbing Contractors

AJAX Plumbing
See Our Display Ad Page 307
   1450 Central Ree 315 729-4000
DUFFY & SONS
   632 Lake Wat 418 274-1234
Landry Plumbing & Heating
   27 Pine Wal 418 829-3600
Reliable Plumbing
   4250 Lawson Wol 315 643-2121

25. What is the phone number of the pizza shop in Pleasantville?
- (A) 315 727-9123
- (B) 315 469-7750
- (C) 315 727-9213
- (D) 315 469-7550

26. Which town in this area has a place to buy plants and flowers?
- (A) Retail
- (B) Centerville
- (C) Remington
- (D) Reedsville

27. What's the telephone number of the plumbing company in Watertown?
- (A) 315 729-4000
- (B) 418 829-3600
- (C) 418 274-1234
- (D) 315 643-2121

28. Where is the Ajax Plumbing Company located?
- (A) On page 307.
- (B) In Remington.
- (C) On Central Ave.
- (D) 315 729-4000.

29. You live in Wallingford, and you need a plumber right away! What number should you call for the closest plumber?
- (A) 315 643-2121
- (B) 418 829-3600
- (C) 418 274-1234
- (D) 315 729-4000

20 (A) (B) (C) (D)   23 (A) (B) (C) (D)   26 (A) (B) (C) (D)   29 (A) (B) (C) (D)
21 (A) (B) (C) (D)   24 (A) (B) (C) (D)   27 (A) (B) (C) (D)
22 (A) (B) (C) (D)   25 (A) (B) (C) (D)   28 (A) (B) (C) (D)

F CLOZE READING: Phone Messages

Choose the correct answers to complete the messages.

Mom [call (A)] [calls (B)] [**called** (●)] at 4:00. She [has (A)] [have (B)] [having (C)] ³⁰ to work late at the

office this evening. [She (A)] [She'll (B)] [She's (C)] ³¹ be home at about 9 PM.

Mr. Slate called [to (A)] [from (B)] [through (C)] ³² the garage about your car repairs. You should call

[us (A)] [her (B)] [him (C)] ³³ as soon as possible.

Grandma and Grandpa called to [speak (A)] [tell (B)] [say (C)] ³⁴ hello. [We're (A)] [They're (B)] [You're (C)] ³⁵

fine, and you don't have to call [them (A)] [they (B)] [their (C)] ³⁶ back.

G LISTENING ASSESSMENT: Recorded Telephone Information

Read and listen to the questions. Then listen to the library's recorded announcements and answer the questions.

37. When does the book club meet?

Ⓐ On the 1st Tuesday of each month.
Ⓑ On the 3rd Tuesday of each month.
Ⓒ On the 1st Thursday of each month.
Ⓓ On the 3rd Thursday of each month.

38. How many evening programs are there each month?

Ⓐ One.
Ⓑ Two.
Ⓒ Three.
Ⓓ Four.

39. How many hours is the library open on Wednesdays?

Ⓐ 4 hours.
Ⓑ 6 hours.
Ⓒ 9 hours.
Ⓓ 12 hours.

40. On which date will the children's story hour meet?

Ⓐ March 5.
Ⓑ March 12.
Ⓒ March 19.
Ⓓ March 26.

H WRITING ASSESSMENT

Write about how you use the telephone. Do you use the telephone for work or for school? Do you talk to family members or friends in other places? Who do you talk to? How often? (Use a separate sheet of paper.)

I SPEAKING ASSESSMENT

I can call someone and answer the phone using these expressions:

Call Answer

☐ ☐ Hello. This is _____. May I please speak to _____?
☐ ☐ _____ isn't here right now. Can I take a message?
☐ ☐ Yes. Please tell _____ that _____.

. . . .

30 Ⓐ Ⓑ Ⓒ Ⓓ   33 Ⓐ Ⓑ Ⓒ Ⓓ   36 Ⓐ Ⓑ Ⓒ Ⓓ   39 Ⓐ Ⓑ Ⓒ Ⓓ

31 Ⓐ Ⓑ Ⓒ Ⓓ   34 Ⓐ Ⓑ Ⓒ Ⓓ   37 Ⓐ Ⓑ Ⓒ Ⓓ   40 Ⓐ Ⓑ Ⓒ Ⓓ

32 Ⓐ Ⓑ Ⓒ Ⓓ   35 Ⓐ Ⓑ Ⓒ Ⓓ   38 Ⓐ Ⓑ Ⓒ Ⓓ

A HOUSEHOLD REPAIR PROBLEMS

Choose the correct answer to complete the conversation.

1. My washing machine is broken.
   You should call _____.
   - Ⓐ a TV repairperson
   - Ⓑ an appliance repairperson
   - Ⓒ an electrician
   - Ⓓ a plumber

2. Somebody stole the keys to my apartment.
   You should call _____.
   - Ⓐ a carpenter
   - Ⓑ a plumber
   - Ⓒ a painter
   - Ⓓ a locksmith

3. Smoke comes into the room when we use
   the fireplace.
   You should call _____.
   - Ⓐ a chimneysweep
   - Ⓑ the fire department
   - Ⓒ a carpenter
   - Ⓓ a painter

4. Channels 2 through 50 are okay, but
   Channels 51 through 100 have a very
   bad picture.
   We should call _____.
   - Ⓐ an electrician
   - Ⓑ an appliance repairperson
   - Ⓒ a TV repairperson
   - Ⓓ the cable TV company

5. Look at all these bugs!
   We should call _____.
   - Ⓐ an electrician
   - Ⓑ the animal control officer
   - Ⓒ an exterminator
   - Ⓓ the zoo

6. I couldn't fix the doorbell.
   Let's call _____.
   - Ⓐ a locksmith
   - Ⓑ an electrician
   - Ⓒ an appliance repairperson
   - Ⓓ a mechanic

B GRAMMAR IN CONTEXT: Securing Household Repair Services

Choose the correct answer to complete the conversation.

7. There's _____ wrong with
   my bathroom sink. Can
   you send _____ to fix it?
   - Ⓐ anything . . . anyone
   - Ⓑ anyone . . . anything
   - Ⓒ something . . . someone
   - Ⓓ someone . . . something

8. I can't send _____ today.
   Will _____ be home
   tomorrow at 10 AM?
   - Ⓐ somebody . . . somebody
   - Ⓑ anybody . . . anything
   - Ⓒ anybody . . . somebody
   - Ⓓ anything . . . something

9. I _____ be home at ten, but
   _____ be back at eleven.
   Is 11:00 okay?
   - Ⓐ won't . . . I'll
   - Ⓑ won't . . . you'll
   - Ⓒ will . . . I'll
   - Ⓓ will . . . you'll

10. Yes. _____ will be there
    at eleven.
    - Ⓐ Anything
    - Ⓑ Anybody
    - Ⓒ Something
    - Ⓓ Someone

READING: A TV Schedule

Look at the TV listings. Choose the correct answer.

	6:00	6:30	7:00	7:30	8:00	8:30	9:00	9:30	10:00	10:30
2	News at 6 (News)	CBS Evening News (News)	Entertainment Tonight (Talk/Tabloid)	Who Wants to be a Millionaire (Game)	Life with Bobby: *Out to Lunch* (Comedy)	Everybody Loves Richard: *The Love Letter* (Comedy)	FBI Special Investigations Unit: *The Dangerous Package* (Crime)		PrimeTime Monday (Talk/Tabloid)	
4	Channel 4 News (News)	NBC Nightly News (News)	EXTRA (Talk/Tabloid)	Access Hollywood (Talk/Tabloid)	Happiest Class: *A New Teacher* (Comedy)	Wanda: *A Visitor from the Past* (Comedy)	Fletcher: *Bob's New Diet* (Comedy)	Fletcher: *Eat Your Vegetables* (Comedy)	Law & Order: *Bad Day at the Bank* (Crime)	
5	Everybody Loves Richard: *The First Day* (Comedy)	Everybody Loves Richard: *A New Friend* (Comedy)	Walt & Grace: *The Argument* (Comedy)	Neighbors: *The Lost Dog* (Comedy)	Biltmore Boys: *Alan's Problem* (Drama)		Three Sisters: *Trisha's New Boss* (Drama)		News at Ten (News)	
7	Eyewitness News (News)	ABC World News Tonight (News)	Jeopardy! (Game)	Wheel of Fortune (Game)	I'm With You: *Lost at the Mall* (Comedy)	Two by Two: *The School Dance* (Comedy)	According to Amy: *The Phone Message* (Comedy)	Better Than Ever: *Jim's New Couch* (Comedy)	LAPD Red: *Fight on the Freeway* (Crime)	
9	Baseball: *Anaheim Angels at Texas Rangers* (Sports) (Live)				KCAL 9 News at 8:00 PM		KCAL 9 News at 9:00 PM		KCAL 9 News at 10:00 PM (News)	Sports Central (News)
11	The Sampsons: *You're Fired!* (Cartoon)	Queen of the Hill: *Sally's New Car* (Comedy)	The Prince of Long Beach: *The Car Accident* (Comedy)	The Sampsons: *Henry's New Job* (Cartoon)	Downtown Medical Center: *Bad Day in the ER* (Reality)		Lost on an Island (Reality)		Fox 11 Ten O'Clock News (News)	
22	Cuanto Cuesta el Show (Game)		Noticias 22 (News)	El Tribunal del Pueblo (Reality)	El Hijo de Pedro Navajas (1986, Spanish)				Noticias 22 (News)	Contacto Deportivo (Sports/Info)
28	The NewsHour (News/Talk)		California's Golden Parks (Nature)	In the Kitchen (Cooking)	This Old Apartment: *Chicago* (Home Repair)		Great Performances: *Boston Symphony Orchestra in Moscow* (Concert)		NOVA: *Bugs, Bugs, Bugs* (Science)	

11. What's on Channel 5 at 7:00?

Ⓐ *EXTRA.*   Ⓒ *Jeopardy!*
Ⓑ *Walt & Grace.*   Ⓓ *Wheel of Fortune.*

12. What time is *Two by Two* on today?

Ⓐ 8:00.   Ⓒ Channel 2.
Ⓑ 8:30.   Ⓓ Channel 7.

13. What's on Channel 2 at 7:30?

Ⓐ A game show.   Ⓒ A news program.
Ⓑ A comedy show.   Ⓓ A cartoon program.

14. Which channel has programs in Spanish?

Ⓐ Channel 5.   Ⓒ Channel 22.
Ⓑ Channel 11.   Ⓓ Channel 28.

15. How many channels show the program *Everybody Loves Richard?*

Ⓐ One.   Ⓒ Three.
Ⓑ Two.   Ⓓ Four.

16. Which channels have news programs at 10:00?

Ⓐ 2, 4, 7.   Ⓒ 5, 9, 11.
Ⓑ 2, 4, 7, 28.   Ⓓ 5, 9, 11, 22.

17. My aunt loves classical music. What time is she going to watch TV today?

Ⓐ 7:00.   Ⓒ 9:00.
Ⓑ 8:00.   Ⓓ 10:00.

18. How many crime shows are on TV this evening?

Ⓐ One.   Ⓒ Three.
Ⓑ Two.   Ⓓ Four.

19. Which channel has the most news programs?

Ⓐ Channel 2.   Ⓒ Channel 7.
Ⓑ Channel 4.   Ⓓ Channel 9.

20. Which program isn't on tonight?

Ⓐ *Neighbors.*   Ⓒ *NOVA.*
Ⓑ *Friends.*   Ⓓ *LAPD Red.*

. . . .

11 Ⓐ Ⓑ Ⓒ Ⓓ   14 Ⓐ Ⓑ Ⓒ Ⓓ   17 Ⓐ Ⓑ Ⓒ Ⓓ   20 Ⓐ Ⓑ Ⓒ Ⓓ

12 Ⓐ Ⓑ Ⓒ Ⓓ   15 Ⓐ Ⓑ Ⓒ Ⓓ   18 Ⓐ Ⓑ Ⓒ Ⓓ

13 Ⓐ Ⓑ Ⓒ Ⓓ   16 Ⓐ Ⓑ Ⓒ Ⓓ   19 Ⓐ Ⓑ Ⓒ Ⓓ    **Go to the next page** ➡

D   CLOZE READING: Household Repairs & Pronoun Review

Choose the correct answers to complete the story.

My brother is very upset. | She   He   We | is having a problem in | him   his   he | ²¹ apartment.
                              Ⓐ   ●   Ⓒ   Ⓐ   Ⓓ   Ⓒ

| He   Him   His | ²² oven is broken. | He   It   She | ²³ doesn't go on. My brother tried to fix it
Ⓐ   Ⓑ   Ⓒ   Ⓐ   Ⓑ   Ⓒ

| itself   hisself   himself | ²⁴, but he couldn't. He called the building manager a few days ago.
Ⓐ   Ⓑ   Ⓒ

| She   Her   Hers | ²⁵ wasn't there, so | it   she   he | ²⁶ left a message on | she   her   hers | ²⁷
Ⓐ   Ⓑ   Ⓒ   Ⓐ   Ⓑ   Ⓒ   Ⓐ   Ⓑ   Ⓒ

answering machine. | He's   His   It's | ²⁸ still waiting for | her   she   hers | ²⁹ to call back. So while
                 Ⓐ   Ⓑ   Ⓒ   Ⓐ   Ⓑ   Ⓒ

my brother's oven is broken, | it   she   he | ³⁰ comes over to | my   me   mine | ³¹ apartment and
                    Ⓐ   Ⓑ   Ⓒ   Ⓐ   Ⓑ   Ⓒ

uses | my   mine   me | ³². I'm happy to help | him   his   he | ³³. After all, he's | me   my   mine | ³⁴
     Ⓐ   Ⓑ   Ⓒ   Ⓐ   Ⓑ   Ⓒ   Ⓐ   Ⓑ   Ⓒ

brother!

E   LISTENING ASSESSMENT: Recorded Telephone Instructions

Read and listen to the questions. Then listen to the telephone instructions and answer the questions.

35. Marina wants to fly from Los Angeles to Madrid, Spain. Which key should she press?

     Ⓐ 1   Ⓒ 3
     Ⓑ 2   Ⓓ 4

36. Roger wants to fly from Houston to Miami. Which key should he press?

     Ⓐ 1   Ⓒ 3
     Ⓑ 2   Ⓓ 4

37. Grace wants to make flight and hotel reservations for a tour of Italy. Which key should she press?

     Ⓐ 1   Ⓒ 3
     Ⓑ 2   Ⓓ 4

38. Daniel is looking for a job as a flight attendant. Which key should he press?

     Ⓐ *   Ⓒ 3
     Ⓑ 1   Ⓓ 5

39. Karen didn't hear the first two instructions. Which key should she press?

     Ⓐ *   Ⓒ 4
     Ⓑ 1   Ⓓ 5

40. Joseph is going to fly to New York tonight. Will his plane leave on time? Which key should he press?

     Ⓐ *   Ⓒ 2
     Ⓑ 1   Ⓓ 5

21 Ⓐ Ⓑ Ⓒ Ⓓ   27 Ⓐ Ⓑ Ⓒ Ⓓ   33 Ⓐ Ⓑ Ⓒ Ⓓ   39 Ⓐ Ⓑ Ⓒ Ⓓ
22 Ⓐ Ⓑ Ⓒ Ⓓ   28 Ⓐ Ⓑ Ⓒ Ⓓ   34 Ⓐ Ⓑ Ⓒ Ⓓ   40 Ⓐ Ⓑ Ⓒ Ⓓ
23 Ⓐ Ⓑ Ⓒ Ⓓ   29 Ⓐ Ⓑ Ⓒ Ⓓ   35 Ⓐ Ⓑ Ⓒ Ⓓ
24 Ⓐ Ⓑ Ⓒ Ⓓ   30 Ⓐ Ⓑ Ⓒ Ⓓ   36 Ⓐ Ⓑ Ⓒ Ⓓ
25 Ⓐ Ⓑ Ⓒ Ⓓ   31 Ⓐ Ⓑ Ⓒ Ⓓ   37 Ⓐ Ⓑ Ⓒ Ⓓ
26 Ⓐ Ⓑ Ⓒ Ⓓ   32 Ⓐ Ⓑ Ⓒ Ⓓ   38 Ⓐ Ⓑ Ⓒ Ⓓ

Go to the next page ⟩

Fill out the chart with your schedule for a typical week. Write in your times at school, at work, at meetings, and at other events. Also write in the things you do to relax, including sports, favorite TV shows, and other evening and weekend activities.

	MON	TUE	WED	THU	FRI	SAT	SUN
6:00 AM							
7:00							
8:00							
9:00							
10:00							
11:00							
12:00 Noon							
1:00 PM							
2:00							
3:00							
4:00							
5:00							
6:00							
7:00							
8:00							
9:00							
10:00							
11:00							

G **SPEAKING ASSESSMENT**

I can ask and answer these questions:

Ask Answer

☐ ☐ When there's something wrong with an appliance in your apartment or home, who fixes it?

☐ ☐ Do you like to fix things?

☐ ☐ What can you fix?

Ask Answer

☐ ☐ Tell about your typical schedule during the week.

☐ ☐ Tell about your typical schedule on the weekend.

☐ ☐ What TV programs do you usually watch? When?

SIDE by SIDE *Plus* Test Prep Workbook 2 Audio Program

The *Side by Side Plus Test Prep Workbook 2* Digital Audio CD contains all listening activities in the unit achievement tests. Teachers can choose to do these activities in class or have students complete them on their own using the audio. The Digital Audio CD also includes MP3 files of the audio program for downloading to a computer or audio player.

Track	Activity
1	Introduction
2	Unit 1: p. 5 Exercise G
3	Unit 2: p. 10 Exercise G
4	Unit 3: p. 14 Exercise H
5	Unit 4: p. 18 Exercise E
6	Unit 5: p. 22 Exercise E
7	Unit 6: p. 26 Exercise G
8	Unit 7: p. 32 Exercise H
9	Unit 8: p. 38 Exercise H
10	Unit 9: p. 42 Exercise G
11	Unit 10: p. 46 Exercise E
12	Unit 11: p. 50 Exercise I
13	Unit 12: p. 54 Exercise G
14	Unit 13: p. 57 Exercise E